PRACTICAL BIDDING AND PRACTICAL PLAY

In the world of bridge, Terence Reese is ranked as Europe's leading authority. A must for all players (or would-be players) PRACTICAL BIDDING leads them simply and explicitly through the intricacies of bidding playing and defending, providing considerable enjoyment en route.

"Undoubtedly my favourite bridge author is Terence Reese, and the pleasure and instruction I have obtained from his books is considerable."

The Portsmouth News

D1198844

PRACTICAL BIDDING
AND
PRACTICAL PLAY

Terence Reese

A STAR BOOK
published by
W. H. ALLEN

A Star Book
Published in 1974
by W. H. Allen & Co. Ltd.
A division of Howard & Wyndham Ltd.
44, Hill Street, London W1X 8LB

First published in Great Britain by
W. H. Allen & Co. Ltd. 1973

Printed in Great Britain by
Richard Clay (The Chaucer Press), Ltd., Bungay, Suffolk

ISBN 0 352 30044 2

Contents of Book I

Contents of Book II

Introduction

Practical Bidding and Practical Play consists of selections from two earlier books, *Play Bridge with Reese* and *Develop Your Bidding Judgment.** The two books go well under the same yoke, for they are similar in format and are aimed at players of the same level. Both describe how an expert thinks at the table and are quite different from the usual textbook.

The play of the cards, happily, does not date, and very few changes have been made in the first book. In the book on bidding it was necessary to rewrite a few paragraphs to fit the modern style, and an occasional postscript has been added. It was interesting for me, after a lapse of years, to study "The Alternatives" and consider what bid I would make now. I freely admit that on occasions my first answer was different from before, but when I read on I generally found that I could be persuaded!

TERENCE REESE

* Also published in a paperback with the title, *Bidding a Bridge Hand*.

Book I
PLAY BRIDGE
WITH
REESE

Foreword to the First Edition

"Mr Reese, how did you know that West had no more hearts?"

"Why did you take that deep finesse in clubs?"

"What made you play for the drop of the King of spades?"

This is the kind of question that the kibitzers fire at the experts after watching a session of play.

As a rule, there is no short answer. From the beginning of a hand a good player tries to play all fifty-two cards—not just the twenty-six he can see. As he goes along he builds up a picture of the opposing hands. That is how he performs the apparent miracles.

In the present book I have tried to show how it is done. The reader sits at my elbow from the moment I pick up my cards and considers how to bid them. (The bids printed in bold face are those which are not only contemplated but actually made.) He follows my thoughts—briefly in the bidding, more fully in the play after the dummy has gone down. In a post-mortem we review the main inferences that have been drawn and extract some general principles.

The setting of the hand is given sometimes as rubber bridge, sometimes as duplicate bridge of one kind or another. The lesson of the hand is usually the same, but the non-tournament player may appreciate a few explanations:

In a team-of-four event there is a comparison of the play between two tables. Scoring and tactics are much the same as in rubber bridge. When there is a big difference between the scores at two tables one side is said to have gained, the other to have lost, a "swing."

In a pairs event the score on each hand obtained by each pair is compared with that of several others who have played the same cards, the principle being that a pair scores one "match point" in respect of every pair whom it outstrips. The pair that does best on a particular hand is said to score a "top," the pair that does worst a "bottom." When a player wants to be safe and get a not-worse-than-average score, he may decide to make the same bid or play as he expects to be made at other tables; he is said to "go with the room."

The first edition of this book contained an acknowledgment to Mrs

Jane Garratt—now Jane Priday, the well-known international player—for her reading of the proofs. That so few criticisms of any substance have been raised over the years is a tribute to her vigilance.

1. Disclosing a Doubleton

"Medium notrump, Stayman responses, and Blackwood?" asked my partner at the beginning of a rubber. Not my favourite methods by any means, but I agree. On the first hand I deal myself the following in the South position:

♠ 10 8 2   ♡ K 10 7 5 2   ◇ K 6   ♣ A K 9

An awkward type of hand because I don't like opening one heart and perhaps, over two diamonds, having to rebid two hearts. Medium notrump, he said; having a couple of tens and a five-card suit I think I'll "borrow" a point or two and open 1NT.

West passes and partner, looking learned, responds **two clubs**, a conventional request for my four-card major. After a pass by East I bid a dutiful **two hearts**. Partner now alarms me with a raise to **six hearts** and all pass. The bidding has been:

South	West	North	East
1NT	pass	2♣	pass
2♡	pass	6♡	pass
pass	pass		

West leads the 9 of spades and partner puts down with pride:

```
                    ♠ A Q
                    ♡ A J 9 8 4
                    ◇ A 8 3
                    ♣ J 7 3
          ♠ 9 led
                    ♠ 10 8 2
                    ♡ K 10 7 5 2
                    ◇ K 6
                    ♣ A K 9
```

Partner has his bid, I suppose, but if he had responded three hearts instead of that idiotic two clubs he would have been playing the hand and we would have avoided this awkward spade lead through the A Q.

(Against any other lead declarer can draw trumps, eliminate diamonds, and play off Ace, King and another club, with various chances.)

I suppose the spade finesse is wrong but it is not unknown for players to underlead a King against a small slam, so I will put in the Queen. East wins with the King and returns the 3, on which West plays the 7. Now, how shall I play the trumps? The only indication I have is that West appears to be short in spades. He led the 9 and I held the 8; with a long suit headed by the 9 7 he would presumably have led low. If anyone is void in hearts, therefore, it is more likely to be East. So I play the 4 of hearts from table; East plays the 6 and I win with the King, West playing the 3. I draw a second trump, West playing the Queen and East discarding a spade.

Somehow I have got to avoid losing a club and superficially the best chance is to find East with Q 10. Before committing myself I must try to find out more about the distribution. I play a diamond to the King and lead the 10 of spades. West discards a club and dummy ruffs.

So East has six spades! I continue with the Ace and another diamond; on the third diamond East plays the 9 and West the 10. The following cards are left:

♠ —
♡ J 9
◇ —
♣ J 7 3

♠ —
♡ 10 7
◇ —
♣ A K 9

I can still enter dummy twice and play East for Q 10 x in clubs, but is that likely? East has six spades, one heart and at least three diamonds. I wonder whether it is four diamonds and two clubs or three diamonds and three clubs. I haven't seen the Jack or Queen of diamonds yet. West played the 10 on the third round, didn't he? Of course! He can't have the Queen and Jack as well, or he would have led a diamond from five to the Q J 10.

Then East must have a doubleton club and my only chance is to drop the Queen. This I am lucky enough to do, for the full hand turns out to be:

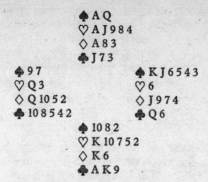

```
              ♠ A Q
              ♡ A J 9 8 4
              ◇ A 8 3
              ♣ J 7 3
♠ 9 7                        ♠ K J 6 5 4 3
♡ Q 3                        ♡ 6
◇ Q 10 5 2                   ◇ J 9 7 4
♣ 10 8 5 4 2                 ♣ Q 6
              ♠ 10 8 2
              ♡ K 10 7 5 2
              ◇ K 6
              ♣ A K 9
```

Partner is sufficiently pleased with the result not to notice that I was under-weight for my medium notrump.

Post-mortem

This was not a difficult hand to play once certain inferences were drawn.

First, West's lead of the 9 of spades from a holding that did not include the 8 suggested that he might be short in spades. That was an indication as to how to play the trump suit, though in practice it would not have mattered had the Ace been led first.

The play of the diamonds, in conjunction with the fact that West had not led a diamond, established that East had at least four cards of the suit.

Then the count became exact. South could tell that he had to play East for Q x in clubs (or Q single) and not for Q 10 x.

2. A Slip in Defence

Playing in a pairs event against average opposition, I hold the following hand:

♠ K 6　♡ A J 8 5 2　♢ 9 7 5 2　♣ 10 2

No one is vulnerable and East, on my right, deals and passes. I pass and West opens **one spade** third in hand. My partner **doubles** and East bids **two spades**. If my King were not in spades I might bid four hearts now, but as it is I think **three hearts** is enough. West passes and partner raises to **four hearts**.

The bidding has gone:

South	West	North	East
—	—	—	pass
pass	1♠	double	2♠
3♡	pass	4♡	pass
pass	pass		

West opens the Queen of diamonds and partner puts down:

```
            ♠ 9 7
            ♡ K Q 10 6
            ♢ A 10 8
            ♣ A K 7 4
♢ Q led
            ♠ K 6
            ♡ A J 8 5 2
            ♢ 9 7 5 2
            ♣ 10 2
```

Somehow I have to avoid losing two diamonds and two spades. I'm not sure what this Queen of diamonds signifies. It could be from Q J and it could be a false card from K Q. At any rate, I don't want to make it easy for East to come in to lead a spade through my King, so for the moment I shall play low from dummy. East plays the 6. As the 4 and 3 are missing, that looks like the beginning of a signal. West continues with the 3 of diamonds. Now I go up with the Ace and East plays the 4, completing an echo.

I am still unsure about the diamonds. West could have Q 3 or Q J 3 or even K Q J 3. K Q 3 is not likely, for then he would have played the King so as not to be thrown in later on. My best hope is that he has led from a doubleton Q 3.

In fact, assuming that West has the Ace of spades I don't see that I stand a chance unless I find him with a doubleton diamond. In that case I may manage some sort of ruff-and-discard elimination if I can eliminate clubs and pass the lead to West with a spade. After making two spade tricks he may have to give me a ruff-and-discard.

To negotiate that I shall want entries to table, and I don't think I should play a round of trumps just yet. I will start with Ace, King and another club. On the third round of clubs East plays the Queen and I ruff with the 8. Now I lead a heart to dummy's Queen, West playing the 4 and East the 3. The position is now:

> ♠ 9 7
> ♡ K 10 6
> ◇ 10
> ♣ 7
>
> ♠ K 6
> ♡ A J 5
> ◇ 9 7
> ♣ —

The Jack of clubs is still out and the elimination I am planning will not succeed unless the trumps are 2 – 2. So I may as well ruff the fourth club and see if both opponents follow to a second heart. West plays the Jack on the fourth club, which is good news, for it suggests that he is short in diamonds. Then both opponents follow to the second round of hearts.

Now I think I'm going to make it if I can duck a spade into West's hand. Is the 7 or the 9 the better card to lead? I think the 7 because if East has something like J 8 x he may be asleep and not put in the 8. So I lead the 7 and East, I am glad to see, plays low. Naturally I do not put in the King, for I don't want West to be able to give his partner the lead on the next trick. West wins with the 8 and heaves a deep sigh. Evidently he is wondering whether to underlead the Ace now. Well, it makes no difference, for if he cashes the Ace of spades he will have to give me a ruff-and-discard on the next lead, the full hand being as follows:

9

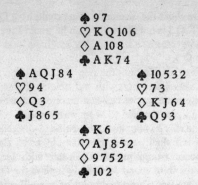

```
                    ♠ 9 7
                    ♡ K Q 10 6
                    ◇ A 10 8
                    ♣ A K 7 4
♠ A Q J 8 4                      ♠ 10 5 3 2
♡ 9 4                           ♡ 7 3
◇ Q 3                           ◇ K J 6 4
♣ J 8 6 5                       ♣ Q 9 3
                    ♠ K 6
                    ♡ A J 8 5 2
                    ◇ 9 7 5 2
                    ♣ 10 2
```

West eventually plays the Ace of spades and surrenders when I show him my remaining cards.

Post-mortem

This contract could have been defeated had East overtaken the Queen of diamonds at trick 1 and returned a spade. The defenders then cash two spade tricks and later make another diamond.

As to declarer's play, it may be noted that an early round of trumps would have been fatal. Suppose that the King of hearts is played from dummy at trick 3. Declarer follows with three rounds of clubs, enters dummy with a second trump and ruffs a fourth club. Now he has only one trump left and if he uses this to enter dummy there will be no trumps for a ruff-and-discard elimination. If South does find himself in this position the best he can do is lead the King of spades from hand. When West wins with the Ace he will have to underlead the Q J to put his partner in with the 10.

3. Short Circuit

In a rubber bridge game of average standard I deal myself the following at game all:

♠ A K 2   ♡ Q 6 4 2   ◇ K J   ♣ A K Q 3

This adds up to 22 points, enough on our system for an opening 2NT, but that does not strike me as at all a good bid with so much strength in the black suits and no tenace combinations. I open **one club.** Partner responds **one diamond** and now I cannot bid less than 3NT. So it has been a simple auction:

South	West	North	East
1♣	pass	1◇	pass
3NT	pass	pass	pass

West leads the 3 of hearts and partner puts down:

♠ 9 5 3
♡ A 8
◇ Q 10 7 6 4
♣ 8 7 4

♡ 3 led

♠ A K 2
♡ Q 6 4 2
◇ K J
♣ A K Q 3

For all our 28 points, this isn't going to be easy if they knock the heart entry out at once. At any rate, I must play low from dummy; East wins with the King and returns the 5 to dummy's Ace.

I can see eight tricks: two spades, two hearts, one diamond and three clubs. No problem if I can induce them to take the Ace of diamonds on the first round. The best chance is to lead the King of diamonds from my hand; if West has A x or A x x he may perhaps put it on.

To enter hand, I play a club to the King. East drops the 2 and West the 6. I lead the King of diamonds now but the result is negative: West plays the 2 and East the 3.

Now it looks as though I haven't got much chance except the club break. I imagine West has led from four hearts and the diamonds may well be 3 – 3 since no one began an echo. If the diamonds are 3 – 3 I wonder whether I can force them to give dummy a diamond trick at the finish. To do that, I have got to eliminate their cards of exit.

I think it might be a good move now to lead and pass a low spade. They will knock out my Queen of hearts and then I can test the clubs. If the clubs don't break I may find one opponent with four clubs and three diamonds, to his disadvantage.

In any event it cannot cost to play a spade. I lead the 2; East wins with the 10 and exits with the 10 of hearts, which I take with the Queen. The situation is now:

```
              ♠ 9 5
              ♡ —
              ◊ Q 10 7
              ♣ 8 4


              ♠ A K
              ♡ 6
              ◊ J
              ♣ A Q 3
```

I cash Ace and King of spades, followed by Ace and Queen of clubs. Now I exit with a diamond and after making his Jack of clubs East has to give the last trick to the table.

This was the full deal:

```
                        ♠ 9 5 3
                        ♡ A 8
                        ◊ Q 10 7 6 4
                        ♣ 8 7 4
     ♠ Q 7 6 4                              ♠ J 10 8
     ♡ J 9 7 3                              ♡ K 10 5
     ◊ 8 5 2                                ◊ A 9 3
     ♣ 10 6                                 ♣ J 9 5 2
                        ♠ A K 2
                        ♡ Q 6 4 2
                        ◊ K J
                        ♣ A K Q 3
```

West started to blame his partner for not cashing the Ace of diamonds when he was in. That would have made no difference, for I could have exited with a club at the finish just as well. East would still have had a diamond left and would have had to play to dummy.

While there is nothing complicated in the play, the ending has to be foreseen in good time. Suppose that after the King of diamonds has held declarer plays a second diamond. East wins this and exits with his 10 of hearts. Now it is too late for South to duck a spade: West can go in with the Queen, cash his good heart and exit in either black suit.

4. An Early Reverse

Playing in a team-of-four match against redoubtable opposition, I pick up the following hand as dealer at game all:

♠ A Q ♡ K J 10 9 7 5 4 ◇ K 3 ♣ K Q

My partner and I play the Acol system in which opening two-bids are forcing for one round. This hand is fairly powerful. However, I don't like to open a two-bid with only one Ace and a suit is that is not solid, so I call simply **one heart.**

After a pass by West partner responds **1NT.** East passes and now, clearly, I can go to **four hearts.**

The bidding has been:

South	West	North	East
1♡	pass	1NT	pass
4♡	pass	pass	pass

West leads the Jack of diamonds and dummy goes down as follows:

> ♠ 10 7 6 4
> ♡ 6 3
> ◇ A Q
> ♣ 10 9 5 4 2

◇ J led

> ♠ A Q
> ♡ K J 10 9 7 5 4
> ◇ K 3
> ♣ K Q

Two Aces to lose, two finesses to take, and I can only be in dummy twice. The question is, which finesse should I take first? That requires a little thought.

Suppose I take the spade finesse first and it loses. I can get back to dummy with the second diamond and finesse in hearts. But one heart finesse may not see me home even if East has the Queen. For example, West might have the singleton Ace and in that case I would need to finesse twice. Alternatively, East might have A Q x; then again I would need to lead through him twice.

It is beginning to look as though the heart finesse should come first. Supposing I finesse the Jack and it fetches the Ace. Then unless West is playing a deep game from A Q or A Q x the Queen will be marked, and when I am next in dummy I can take another finesse in hearts. So long as I lose only one heart it will not matter about the spades, so I'll take the heart finesse first.

I win the first trick with the Queen of diamonds and lead the 3 of hearts from the table. East plays the 8 and I put in the Jack, which holds, West playing the 2. It looks as though East has A Q 8. I think I have played it the right way, giving myself the chance of two heart leads. I play the King of diamonds to dummy's Ace and lead another heart from the table.

Disaster! East discards a diamond on the second heart and West wins with the Queen. West cashes the Ace of hearts and exits with a diamond, which I ruff. I am now in this unenviable position:

♠ 10 7 6
♡ —
♢ —
♣ 10 9 5 4

♠ A Q
♡ K 10 9
♢ —
♣ K Q

This is most humiliating because I am sure the spade finesse is right all the time. The only remaining hope is that they let me slip through a club and bring off some sort of three-card end-play. I try the Queen of clubs. As expected, East takes it with the Ace and returns a small club. Now I must go through the motions of leading out my hearts. But the story has no happy ending—at least not for me. I have to surrender the last trick to the King of spades and my worst fears are confirmed when the hand turns out to be:

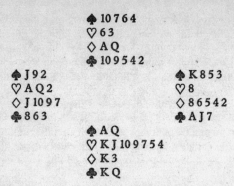

```
              ♠ 10 7 6 4
              ♡ 6 3
              ◇ A Q
              ♣ 10 9 5 4 2
♠ J 9 2                        ♠ K 8 5 3
♡ A Q 2                        ♡ 8
◇ J 10 9 7                     ◇ 8 6 5 4 2
♣ 8 6 3                        ♣ A J 7
              ♠ A Q
              ♡ K J 10 9 7 5 4
              ◇ K 3
              ♣ K Q
```

With murder in my heart I congratulate West on his good defence.

Post-mortem

I trust that the reader has not missed the point of this deal: if West had taken the Jack of hearts with the Queen, then when next in dummy I would have taken the spade finesse and made the contract.

West might also have tried to deceive me by winning the first heart with the Ace. (If he had had A Q alone that would have been a brilliant play.) You may remember that I did envisage the possibility of West winning with the Ace when he had the A Q. Somehow he caught me napping by ducking on that first trick.

The defence followed a sound general principle, that when declarer takes an early finesse in a critical suit it is generally good play to hold up. This applies both to a side suit and to the trump suit. The value of such defence is twofold: it causes declarer to misplace the cards and may induce him, as on the present hand, to expend an entry from dummy on a useless cause.

5. A Revealing Cover

Playing rubber bridge with a somewhat stolid partner against reasonably strong opponents I hold the following:

♠ Q 7 3   ♡ Q J 10 6 4   ◇ A 5 2   ♣ A J

Neither side is vulnerable and West, on my left, deals and opens **one club**. That is passed by North and East and I reopen with **one heart**. West passes and my partner gives me **two hearts**.

There are three possible calls at this moment. Some players would say that I had a maximum for a bid of one (as opposed to a double) in the protective position and that I should go straight to four hearts. There are too many losers for that and anyway I am not sure it will be the best contract. As I see it, the choice is between 2NT and three hearts. With my present partner I shall make the most straightforward bid: **three hearts**. Partner raises this to **four hearts** after some thought. The bidding has been:

South	West	North	East
—	1♣	pass	pass
1♡	pass	2♡	pass
3♡	pass	4♡	pass
pass	pass		

West leads the Queen of diamonds and partner, remarking that he was thinking of 3NT, puts down:

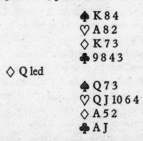

```
                    ♠ K 8 4
                    ♡ A 8 2
                    ◇ K 7 3
                    ♣ 9 8 4 3
◇ Q led
                    ♠ Q 7 3
                    ♡ Q J 10 6 4
                    ◇ A 5 2
                    ♣ A J
```

Yes, 3NT would have been better, especially played from my hand.

Prospects are not too good in four hearts. Even if the heart finesse is right I have four apparent losers.

Dummy plays low on the first trick, East plays the 6 and I win. Now can it make any difference which heart I lead? If I lead the 10 and West puts in the King it will be fair to assume that it's a singleton, whereas if I lead the Queen and West puts on the King that won't tell me anything. So I lead the 10 and West does play the King. I put on the Ace from dummy and return the 2. If I am going to play East for the 9 7 5 3 I've got to finesse at once. Surely West couldn't have put in the King from a doubleton? No, I'm going to finesse the 6.

The 6 holds and East looks aggrieved. I follow with the Queen of hearts and then the Jack to draw East's last trump. West, meanwhile, has had to make three discards. The first is the 6 of clubs. the second the 5 of spades and the third, after much thought, the 9 of diamonds. I have to discard from dummy on the fourth trump. I don't want to let a spade or a club go, for they exercise some sort of threat against West, so I discard dummy's 7 of diamonds. The following cards are left:

♠ K 8 4
♡ —
♢ K
♣ 9 8 4 3

♠ Q 7 3
♡ 4
♢ 5 2
♣ A J

I have a fairly good picture of West's hand. He has let one club go, so I place him with five clubs. He let one spade go quite gaily but would not release a second; that looks like A J x x or A 10 x x. One heart I know of and his diamonds were presumably Q J 9, for he led the Queen and has played the 9.

I think the game now must be to extract his diamond and duck a club into his hand. East may well have a club honour (since the King of clubs was not led) and in that case dummy's 9 8 of clubs may assume some significance. So in the diagram position I lead a diamond to the King, on which West plays the Jack, and return a club, finessing the Jack and losing to West's King.

West returns a club on which East's Queen falls. Now dummy's 9 8 of clubs are equals against the 10 and I can make the contract in several ways. I lead a spade to the King and return the 9 of clubs, discarding my losing diamond. Now West must either lead into my Queen of spades or concede a trick to dummy's 8 of clubs. There was no defence, the full hand being as follows:

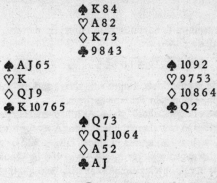

```
              ♠ K 8 4
              ♡ A 8 2
              ◇ K 7 3
              ♣ 9 8 4 3
♠ A J 6 5                    ♠ 10 9 2
♡ K                         ♡ 9 7 5 3
◇ Q J 9                     ◇ 10 8 6 4
♣ K 10 7 6 5                ♣ Q 2
              ♠ Q 7 3
              ♡ Q J 10 6 4
              ◇ A 5 2
              ♣ A J
```

Post-mortem

That lead of the 10 of trumps is worth noting. In such situations it is generally possible to gauge whether the defender has the King alone or K x. As the hand turned out, East would have done better to insert the 7 of hearts on the second round, forcing me to use an entry to dummy early on.

Note, also, how from West's three discards on the trumps it was possible to assess his exact distribution. That made it safe to release the King of diamonds. West could not discard in any other way. If he had let go a second club, for example, South would have led out Ace and Jack and would have established the fourth club in dummy.

6. Trial and Error

Playing in a team-of-four match with an expert partner, I hold the following as dealer:

♠ Q 8 3 ♡ A J 9 7 6 3 ◇ 6 ♣ A Q 4

Neither side is vulnerable. I open **one heart** and my partner raises to **two hearts.** The opponents remain silent.

Rather close whether I should go on. As it happens, my partner and I have lately agreed to play short-suit trial bids. (A try for game by South at this point, such as two spades or three clubs, would be a trial bid.) The idea is that when a player makes a trial bid he should choose a short suit—as a rule, a singleton. That will help partner to judge whether or not the hands fit well.

As this is a borderline hand I think I might give this convention a try-out. I bid **three diamonds.** Partner jumps to **four hearts** and all pass.

So the bidding has been:

South	West	North	East
1♡	pass	2♡	pass
3◇	pass	4♡	pass
pass	pass		

West leads the King of diamonds and, proudly remarking that he has remembered the convention, partner puts down:

```
                    ♠ J 7 2
                    ♡ K 10 5 2
                    ◇ 9 5 4
                    ♣ K 10 6
◇ K led
                    ♠ Q 8 3
                    ♡ A J 9 7 6 3
                    ◇ 6
                    ♣ A Q 4
```

I see that I am in some danger of losing a diamond and three spades,

20

not to mention a possible heart, but I don't blame the convention: we both forced the pace a little and there is some duplication in clubs.

East plays the 8 of diamonds on the first trick. West continues with the 7 of diamonds, East plays the Ace and I ruff. The first point to consider is which opponent, if either, is likely to have three hearts to the Queen.

So far as one can judge from the play of the diamonds, West is slightly more likely to have length. His play of the King followed by the 7 could well be from a five- or six-card suit. I should imagine that the spade honours are divided, for West appears to have K Q of diamonds and East the A J. If either had A K of spades as well, he might have entered the bidding. Now, if West had a void heart together with a diamond suit and a high honour in spades, he would perhaps have come in over one heart.

I don't think actually that either opponent is void of hearts. I am not going to spend more time on this. I lay down the Ace and all is well. Both follow.

When I lead a second heart, West plays the Queen and North the King, East discarding the 3 of diamonds.

So much for that, but the main battle is still ahead: avoiding the loss of three spade tricks. If either opponent held A K I could lead through him, but I am still disposed to think the honours are divided. Then could either player have a doubleton honour? For example, if West had K x or A x I could lead from hand towards the Jack and duck on the way back. Again I don't think it's likely since they might well have manoeuvred to take a spade ruff if the distribution were 5 – 2; also, on the second heart East discarded a diamond, and if he had held five spades he would probably have thrown a spade.

I am coming more and more to the conclusion that it cannot be done by brute force. If the spades are 4 – 3 and the honours are divided my only chance is to induce a misplay. I'll lead the Jack of spades from dummy and hope that East does not play the Ace or King. The sooner I do it the better.

On the Jack of spades East plays low. Better! West wins with the King and plays a third diamond. I can shorten it now: I cross to dummy in clubs and lead another spade from table. East plays the Ace and the rest are mine.

While West is having his say about his partner's failure to play the Ace of spades on the Jack, let us look at the full deal:

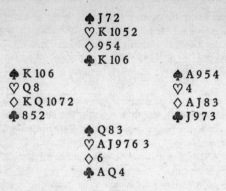

$\spadesuit$ J 7 2
$\heartsuit$ K 10 5 2
$\diamondsuit$ 9 5 4
$\clubsuit$ K 10 6

$\spadesuit$ K 10 6 $\spadesuit$ A 9 5 4
$\heartsuit$ Q 8 $\heartsuit$ 4
$\diamondsuit$ K Q 10 7 2 $\diamondsuit$ A J 8 3
$\clubsuit$ 8 5 2 $\clubsuit$ J 9 7 3

$\spadesuit$ Q 8 3
$\heartsuit$ A J 9 7 6 3
$\diamondsuit$ 6
$\clubsuit$ A Q 4

Post-mortem

There were a number of small indications on this hand of a sort that are liable to be overlooked. The fact that the high diamonds were divided between the two hands, taken in conjunction with the fact that neither opponent entered the bidding, suggested that the spade honours would also be divided. Also, the fact that the opponents had not taken a ruff in spades suggested that they were not 5 – 2.

It should be mentioned that the lengthy reflection about the spades took place after the second trick and not when declarer was in dummy with the King of hearts. The narrative of the play was differently arranged for convenience.

As to the defence, presumably East placed South with some such holding as K 10 x x in spades. His failure to play the Ace on the Jack was a mistake but not such on unlikely one. Note that the defence would have been easier had South played off three rounds of clubs before leading the spade Jack. Then East would have known that the defence had to take three spade tricks and would surely have covered the Jack.

7. Pre-emptive Aid

In a game of rubber bridge against strong and enterprising opposition I hold the following hand in second position:

♠ 86 ♡ A 108732 ♢ A 2 ♣ A J 4

Both sides are vulnerable and East, on my right, deals and opens **three diamonds**. It's just as well I don't play the convention in which an overcall in the next higher ranking suit would not show hearts at all but would be for a take-out. Although vulnerable, I must risk **three hearts**. After a pass by West my partner raises to **four hearts** and all pass.

So the bidding has gone:

South	West	North	East
—	—	—	3♢
3♡	pass	4♡	pass
pass	pass		

West leads the 4 of diamonds. Remarking, "I haven't much for you," partner puts down:

♠ A Q 7 4
♡ Q 9 4
♢ 9 7 6
♣ 8 5 2

♢ 4 led

♠ 8 6
♡ A 10 8 7 3 2
♢ A 2
♣ A J 4

The lead looks like a singleton, though it could possibly be from a doubleton, East having opened on a six-card suit with 100 honours. At any rate, I cannot risk having my Ace ruffed, so I play the 6 from dummy and win the 10 with the Ace.

Prospects are not too good. It looks like a diamond and two clubs to lose, apart from the spades and hearts. There are two slender chances of not losing a heart: I can play West for the singleton Jack, leading the Queen from dummy, or East for the singleton King. In view of East's pre-emptive bid, the better chance must be to play him for the singleton, so I lay down the Ace of hearts, on which West plays the Jack and East the 5. Have I done the wrong thing? No, West's Jack was not single. On the next round he plays the King and East the 6.

West now switches to the Jack of spades through dummy's A Q. I finesse and the Queen holds. West's 4 of diamonds was obviously a singleton. I don't know yet whether I can do anything about the clubs, but I'm going to play off Ace and another spade to build up a picture of the hand. All follow to the Ace of spades and on the next round East plays the 10. I ruff and West drops the King. There are now seven cards left and I have lost only one trick:

♠ 7
♡ 9
♦ 9 7
♣ 8 5 2

♠ —
♡ 10 8 7
♦ 2
♣ A J 4

The 9 of spades is still out and no doubt West has it. What was his hand exactly? Two hearts and one diamond I know; four spades and six clubs, that must be it. Some light is beginning to appear. I can cross to dummy's 9 of hearts and throw West in with a spade, forcing him to lead clubs for what that is worth. If West's clubs are headed by the K Q I can play an old-fashioned Bath Coup and make him lead into my A J.

But can his clubs be as good as six to the K Q? True, he wouldn't have bid four clubs over three hearts but he might well have doubled four hearts, Also, he would probably have led the King of clubs at some point.

It is beginning to look as though East has the singleton King or Queen. In that event it is no use crossing to dummy and playing a spade, for West will exit perforce with a low club. If I have the picture right the Ace of clubs will drop the singleton King or Queen and then I can go for the end-play.

So in the diagram position I play off the Ace of clubs. East, I am glad to see, plays the Queen. Then I cross to dummy and lead the 7 of spades, discarding my 2 of diamonds. West wins with the 9, cashes the King of clubs and concedes the last trick to my Jack. I just make the contract, losing a spade (when I threw the diamond), a heart and a club.

This was the full hand:

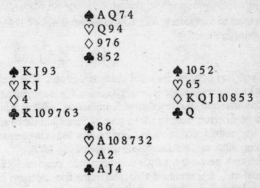

♠ A Q 7 4
♡ Q 9 4
♢ 9 7 6
♣ 8 5 2

♠ K J 9 3   ♠ 10 5 2
♡ K J   ♡ 6 5
♢ 4   ♢ K Q J 10 8 5 3
♣ K 10 9 7 6 3   ♣ Q

♠ 8 6
♡ A 10 8 7 3 2
♢ A 2
♣ A J 4

Post-mortem

As often happens, East's weak pre-emptive bid pushed us into a game that we might not otherwise have reached and might not have made. A perceptive reader may have noted that there was another quite elegant way to make the contract. After ruffing the third spade and cashing the Ace of clubs South can exit with a diamond. East wins and plays another diamond on which South discards a club. Then East must concede a ruff and discard.

Weak pre-emptive bids undoubtedly make the play easy for the opponents when they gain the declaration. I hold strongly to the view that in rubber bridge especially it pays to vary one's three bids, making them often on two to three quick tricks. A pre-empt that is known to be weak is a blunt sword.

8. High Pressure

In a team of four match, with both sides vulnerable, I hold the following third in hand:

$$\spadesuit\ 52 \quad \heartsuit\ 1054 \quad \diamondsuit\ A\ 105 \quad \clubsuit\ KJ632$$

North, my partner, deals and opens **two clubs**. That is the conventional forcing bid in our system, promising a game or near-game hand. With a five-card suit, together with an Ace and a King, I have enough for a positive response, so after a pass by East I bid **three clubs**. With the opponents remaining silent, my partner bids **three spades**. I have nothing more to show for the moment, so I bid **3NT**.

Partner's next call is a little unexpected: he raises to 5NT. That is a natural call, I presume. We do play some five notrump conventions but only when a suit has been clearly agreed. He knows I have a club suit and I cannot support his spades, so my natural call is **6NT**.

The full bidding:

South	West	North	East
—	—	2♣	pass
3♣	pass	3♠	pass
3NT	pass	5NT	pass
6NT	pass	pass	pass

West leads the 7 of spades and partner puts down:

$$\spadesuit\ AQJ983$$
$$\heartsuit\ AK7$$
$$\diamondsuit\ KQ$$
$$\clubsuit\ A8$$

♠ 7 led

$$\spadesuit\ 52$$
$$\heartsuit\ 1054$$
$$\diamondsuit\ A\ 105$$
$$\clubsuit\ KJ632$$

My partner's 5NT was a good call, in my opinion. Certainly we are in the best contract.

If I can make five tricks in the spade suit, that will be enough, except that there may be entry trouble. I wonder what that lead of the 7 means, through dummy's suit. Is anything to be gained by putting up the Ace? Only if East has the singleton King, and I don't think it is likely that West would have led from 10 x x x. If the spades are all on the wrong side I shall have to make the tricks from clubs. For the moment, I will put in the Jack and see what happens.

On the Jack of spades East throws a diamond. Pity I didn't finesse the 8 of spades; I might have done, at that. Now I can't make more than three spade tricks. Three spades, two hearts and three diamonds make eight, so on the surface four club tricks will see me home, but it's not so simple as that. Entries are a problem. Suppose I play Ace of clubs, finesse the Jack and find East with Q x x x. I can set up a fifth club but I'll have to overtake one of dummy's diamonds in order to enter hand.

The difficult question is whether or not to play off the K Q of diamonds before taking the club finesse. If the clubs are 3 – 3 and West has the Queen it is essential to keep the diamond entry to my hand. On the other hand, since the spades are 5 – 0 it is more likely (a) that East will have the Queen of clubs, and (b) that the clubs will break 4 – 2 or worse.

Suppose I play off the diamonds and the Ace of clubs and successfully finesse the Jack of clubs: how do I stand then? Counting three tricks in spades, that will give me eleven tricks on top. And surely West will be in some trouble, for he won't be able to let a spade go.

I find these chances hard to estimate and I haven't considered the extra possibility that the Jack of diamonds might fall in two rounds. I am going to take the simple view that if the club finesse is right I shall surely be able to exert pressure on West. I play off the K Q of diamonds and everyone follows. Since East threw a diamond on the first trick I assume he began with at least five, very likely six. Now I play Ace of clubs and finesse the Jack of clubs. That passes off all right, West playing the 10 on the second round. I play the King of clubs and West throws a heart. The hand is developing much as I expected. The following cards are left:

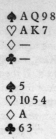

♠ A Q 9 8
♡ A K 7
◇ —
♣ —

♠ 5
♡ 10 5 4
◇ A
♣ 6 3

West has four spades still left and I am pretty sure I have him now. If he follows to the Ace of diamonds his other two cards will be a couple of hearts. Let's put that to the test. On the Ace of diamonds West throws the 8 of hearts. Now it's a certainty. I throw a heart from table, finesse the Queen of spades and cash the top hearts. Dummy's last three cards are the A 9 8 of spades and West has K 10 6. Like a well brought up chess player, West resigns, not waiting for the inevitable end-play. This was the full hand:

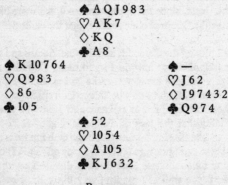

♠ A Q J 9 8 3
♡ A K 7
◇ K Q
♣ A 8

♠ K 10 7 6 4
♡ Q 9 8 3
◇ 8 6
♣ 10 5

♠ —
♡ J 6 2
◇ J 9 7 4 3 2
♣ Q 9 7 4

♠ 5 2
♡ 10 5 4
◇ A 10 5
♣ K J 6 3 2

Post-mortem

The long spades in dummy were like a tin can attached to West's tail. Declarer had to foresee the possibility of exerting pressure on West in spades and hearts. As was remarked in the narrative, playing off the K Q of diamonds at an early stage, giving up the diamond entry to the South hand, would have been a mistake if West had had Q x x of clubs. It became the right play once declarer realized that three tricks in diamonds plus three in clubs would put him in a commanding position.

9. . . . But the Patient Died

In a hotly contested game of rubber bridge I hold the following in third position:

♠ A Q 6   ♡ Q 8 5 2   ♢ 10 8 6 3   ♣ A 10

With both sides vulnerable, my partner deals and opens **one club**. In such positions I hold strongly to the natural and uninformative 2NT rather than the scientific approach of one diamond or one heart. So I respond **2NT** and partner bids **three clubs**. That is a weak bid in our system and strictly I ought to pass. However, he has opened vulnerable and I have the Ace of his suit. I shall have to take the blame if it goes wrong, but I'm going to battle on with **3NT**. All pass, so bidding has been:

South	West	North	East
—	—	1♣	pass
2NT	pass	3♣	pass
3NT	pass	pass	pass

West leads the King of diamonds, and muttering, "I did warn you," partner puts down:

```
              ♠ 10
              ♡ A J 10
              ◇ J 7
              ♣ K J 9 6 4 3 2
  ◇ K led
              ♠ A Q 6
              ♡ Q 8 5 2
              ◇ 10 8 6 3
              ♣ A 10
```

They can't run more than four diamonds against me, so this is going to depend on the Queen of clubs at worst. West's King of diamonds holds the first trick and he follows with the 2 of diamonds to his partner's Ace. East returns a diamond and I try the 8 but West wins with the 9 and cashes the Queen. Meanwhile, I have to discard twice

29

from the table. There are more hazards to this contract than I realized at first. I have got to rely on making seven club tricks, so I throw two hearts from dummy, leaving the Ace bare. On the last diamond East throws the 4 of hearts.

West, inevitably, leads the 7 of hearts, taking dummy's Ace off the table. East plays the 3, completing an echo. I lead a club to the Ace and the 10 back. No Queen appears, so now I have to work out whether or not to finesse, with about 1000 points depending on it.

All I know for certain is that West began with four diamonds. As to the hearts, I can't be altogether sure but the indications are that they are 4 – 2. If East had had only three hearts he would probably have discarded a spade rather than a heart either from three small or from K x x. If West has four diamonds and two hearts, is he likely to have a doubleton club? With five spades he might surely have led a spade. These inferences are not very secure but I can't think of anything better. I'm going to play the Jack.

East produces the Queen and partner fixes me with a steely glare. East now leads the Jack of spades, pinning dummy's 10.

Every trick costs money, so I must get out of this as best I can. I still think that West began with short hearts. If so, the reason why he didn't lead a spade from a five-card suit may be that it was headed by the King and he preferred to lead from K Q 9 x of diamonds. If West has the King of hearts as well—that echo by East doesn't mean anything— I may still emerge with a few tricks. So I'm not going to finesse the spade now. After the Ace has won, the following cards are left:

♠ —
♡ —
◇ —
♣ K 9 6 4 3

♠ Q 6
♡ Q 8 5
◇ —
♣ —

There are three hearts still out—the King, the 9 and the 6. If the King is held by East I probably shan't make another trick anyway. If West has K 6 left and East the 9 I do better to play the Queen, keeping East out of the lead. West will throw me back with a heart and I shall make two more tricks that way. On the other hand, if West has the

King of hearts alone I can make three more tricks if I exit with a low heart now. That is just as likely, so I lead the 5. West has to put the King on this: he makes his King of spades and I win the last three tricks. That's 300 away, not so brilliant when one looks at the full hand:

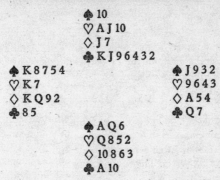

♠ 10
♡ A J 10
◇ J 7
♣ K J 9 6 4 3 2

♠ K 8 7 5 4   ♠ J 9 3 2
♡ K 7   ♡ 9 6 4 3
◇ K Q 9 2   ◇ A 5 4
♣ 8 5   ♣ Q 7

♠ A Q 6
♡ Q 8 5 2
◇ 10 8 6 3
♣ A 10

"It might have been worse," I begin to tell my partner. "For example, if I finesse the Queen of spades all I make is my three Aces and . . ." But he isn't listening.

Post-mortem

Declarer could have protected himself from disaster on this hand by discarding a couple of clubs on the long diamonds instead of the J 10 of hearts. That would be somewhat cowardly play, however, for to make the contract he would still have to find the Queen of clubs as well as the heart finesse. Despite the result, the play was well thought out. The operation was successful but the patient died.

10. Delayed Entry

My partner in this hand of rubber bridge is a player with whom I have small acquaintance. The opponents I know well to be strong and enterprising players. Early in the rubber, neither side having scored below the line, I pick up as dealer:

♠ K ♡ A Q 10 3 ◇ Q 10 8 5 ♣ K 7 6 4

I open **one heart**, West passes and my partner responds **two diamonds**. East comes in with **two spades** and I support my partner to **three diamonds**. After a pass by West North reverts to **three hearts**, which East passes. The bidding so far:

South	West	North	East
1♡	pass	2◇	2♠
3◇	pass	3♡	pass
?			

I don't know if he intends this sequence to be forcing or not. The hand could play awkwardly in hearts if he had only three trumps, so I am certainly not going four hearts. The question is whether I should leave it in three hearts or put him back to four diamonds. If his diamonds are not good he may return to four hearts, which will probably be doubled. In fact, I rather distrust the whole affair. I am going to pass although, technically, the right bid is probably four diamonds.

But West is still there and he reopens with **three spades**. Partner is nodding his head and looking serious. Eventually he bids **four hearts** and to my relief no one doubles. The full bidding has been:

South	West	North	East
1♡	pass	2◇	2♠
3◇	pass	3♡	pass
pass	3♣	4♡	pass
pass	pass		

West leads the Ace of spades and with well-founded apprehension partner puts down:

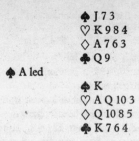

```
            ♠ J 7 3
            ♡ K 9 8 4
            ◇ A 7 6 3
            ♣ Q 9
♠ A led
            ♠ K
            ♡ A Q 10 3
            ◇ Q 10 8 5
            ♣ K 7 6 4
```

I suppose he thought he wasn't good enough to give me three hearts on the first round. When the spades were supported he placed me with a singleton. A scientific sort of player, I can see that.

After the Ace of spades West continues with the 9 and I ruff with the 3 of hearts. Since no one doubled I think I can assume that the hearts are going to break 3 – 2. I shall have to ruff spades twice, so I can't draw trumps yet awhile. I must force out the Ace of clubs first.

On the lead of the 4 of clubs West plays the 3, dummy the Queen and East the Ace. East returns the Queen of spades. As West supported spades I imagine he has three, so I trump with the 10 and West follows suit. Now I draw Ace and Queen of hearts and on the second round East drops the Jack. That leaves the cards as follows:

```
            ♠ —
            ♡ K 9
            ◇ A 7 6 3
            ♣ 9

            ♠ —
            ♡ —
            ◇ Q 10 8 5
            ♣ K 7 6
```

Sooner or later I have to develop the diamonds to lose only one trick. The simplest line is to enter dummy with the Ace of diamonds, draw the last trump and lead a low diamond, hoping that East has a doubleton honour. Before I do that, let me see if I can reconstruct the hand.

East surely has six spades and a doubleton heart, unless that Jack of hearts was a peculiar false card. He could have a doubleton diamond and three clubs to the Ace. Alternatively, he could have one diamond and four clubs. I can't see any strong clue from his bidding or play.

What about West? Could he have, for example,

♠ A x x   ♡ x x x   ◇ J x x   ♣ J x x x ?

He would pass three diamonds on that but would he reopen with three spades? Unlikely. Similarly, with a diamond more and a club less, he would probably pass three hearts.

He must have thought he had good defence against four hearts—I am sure that is the explanation. He must have reckoned on tricks in diamonds, probably holding K J x or even K J x x. If that's so I cannot lose by leading the Queen of diamonds from hand. I may as well do that at once while I have the trumps and clubs under some control.

On the Queen of diamonds West plays low and East drops the 9. On that play West could have K x x and East J 9 but I feel it is more probable that West has K J x x and East the singleton 9. Either way, it is safe for me to lead another diamond (unless East has the third trump all the time). I lead the 5 of diamonds, West plays low again and I put in the 6 from table. This holds the trick, East discarding a spade. Now I draw the trump and lose only to the King of diamonds. This was the full hand:

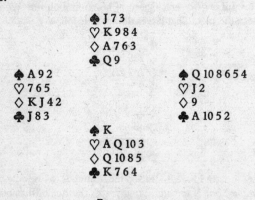

```
                    ♠ J 7 3
                    ♡ K 9 8 4
                    ◇ A 7 6 3
                    ♣ Q 9
♠ A 9 2                            ♠ Q 10 8 6 5 4
♡ 7 6 5                            ♡ J 2
◇ K J 4 2                          ◇ 9
♣ J 8 3                            ♣ A 10 5 2
                    ♠ K
                    ♡ A Q 10 3
                    ◇ Q 10 8 5
                    ♣ K 7 6 4
```

Post-mortem

After the Queen of diamonds held, declarer could also have played King of clubs, ruffed a club and drawn the last trump. Then a small diamond from table would leave West on play. That line of play would fail, however, if West had three diamonds and four clubs.

The main point of the play was the lead of the Queen of diamonds in the diagram position instead of the lazy play of a low diamond to the Ace. West, it will be remembered, passed three diamonds and then came late into the bidding with three spades. When a player follows such a sequence it is usually possible to define his hand within fairly close limits.

11. Something up my Sleeve

Playing in a pairs contest against expert opponents, I hold:

♠ A K J 9 6 5 4 ♡ J 10 3 ◇ 10 4 ♣ 5

With both sides vulnerable, my partner, North, opens **1NT** and East passes. This would be a good hand for Texas. Playing the Texas convention, I would bid four diamonds and my partner would transfer to four spades. It might well be better that he, the notrump bidder, should play the hand in spades.

However, we have not agreed to play Texas, so that possibility does not arise. I might bid three spades and pass if partner rebid 3NT. That could produce a good match-point score but it is the sort of bid that I would try only if I were desperate for a "top." As it is, I shall bid a straightforward **four spades**. Everyone passes, so the bidding has been simple:

South	West	North	East
—	—	1NT	pass
4♠	pass	pass	pass

West leads the Jack of clubs and partner puts down:

♠ Q 7 2
♡ A Q 6 4
◇ K 6 5
♣ A K 6

♣ J led

♠ A K J 9 6 5 4
♡ J 10 3
◇ 10 4
♣ 5

That's a friendly lead. I cannot fail to make eleven tricks, for at most I shall lose a heart and a diamond. To make a good score, I may need two overtricks. If the King of hearts is wrong, how can I stop East from playing a diamond?

It would be foolish to play off two top clubs and throw a diamond.

If I have to lose a heart I want to do that before the enemy can sum up the situation. To begin with, I win the first club with the Ace and come to hand with a spade, on which East plays the 10 and West the 3.

Now if I lead the 10 or Jack of hearts and East wins with the King he will see that there is not much future for the defence and will play a diamond even if he has the Ace himself, sitting over the King. He is that sort of player.

I think I can make it more difficult for him by leading my 3 of hearts. I won't help him to count the hand by playing off a second round of spades. On the 3 of hearts West plays the 5, dummy the Queen and East the King. This is the critical moment. If East does not have the Ace of diamonds he will certainly play one, but if he has the Ace he may not realize that he must make it now or never.

Better! East returns a club. I ruff, draw the second trump, cash J 10 of hearts and cross to dummy's Queen of spades. Then my two losing diamonds go away on the Ace of hearts and the King of clubs and I end up with twelve tricks for what should be a good score.

This was the full deal:

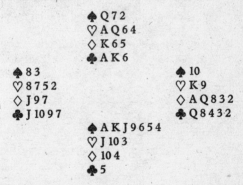

```
              ♠ Q 7 2
              ♡ A Q 6 4
              ◇ K 6 5
              ♣ A K 6
  ♠ 8 3                      ♠ 10
  ♡ 8 7 5 2                  ♡ K 9
  ◇ J 9 7                    ◇ A Q 8 3 2
  ♣ J 10 9 7                 ♣ Q 8 4 3 2
              ♠ A K J 9 6 5 4
              ♡ J 10 3
              ◇ 10 4
              ♣ 5
```

Post-mortem

This hand is instructive in the sense that players of different degree would play it in a number of different ways. A weak player would hastily take the discard on the second club and after that the defenders could not fail to cash their diamond when they won a heart. A better player would avoid that pitfall but would probably draw two trumps and then run the 10 of hearts. An average defender in East's position might still fail to cash the Ace of diamonds, but not a good defender, for he would see that South had seven tricks in spades, two in clubs and at least two in hearts. That being so, he would cash the Ace of diamonds—a play that could lose only if South were void in diamonds.

With regard to the line of play actually followed, a good technician may not have noted that leading the 3 of hearts destroys certain squeeze possibilities should West have K 9 x x of hearts and Ace of diamonds. With that holding, West can be squeezed in the red suits so long as South does not block the run of the hearts by leading the 3 originally. Even then, the situation can be restored if South is allowed to slip through the 10 on the next round. Setting one chance against the other, I still think that the deceptive lead of the 3 is more likely to bring in the extra trick.

12. A Hail of Bullets

Playing rubber bridge with a somewhat excitable partner, I hold the following second in hand:

♠ Q 84   ♡ A K J 6 3   ◇ 84   ♣ A Q 5

No one is vulnerable and East, on my right, deals and passes. I open **one heart** and West overcalls with **four spades**. Never one to be shut out, my partner bids **five diamonds** and East **doubles**. I pass, so does West, and partner now retreats to **five hearts**. East **doubles** again, surprising no one. All pass. The bidding has gone:

South	West	North	East
—	—	—	pass
1♡	4♠	5◇	double
pass	pass	5♡	double
pass	pass	pass	

West leads the King of spades and partner's hand is not encouraging:

```
              ♠ 3
              ♡ Q 9 2
              ◇ K Q 10 6 3 2
              ♣ K J 10
♠ K led
              ♠ Q 8 4
              ♡ A K J 6 3
              ◇ 8 4
              ♣ A Q 5
```

I don't think I'm going to enjoy this. On the first spade East plays the 5. West switches to the 9 of clubs, which I win in dummy with the 10, East playing the 2.

There is a slight reason for leaving the lead in dummy. I am going to play a diamond next, for no doubt East has the Ace, and by leading from dummy I force East to play before his partner. If I lead from my hand and West has a doubleton, he will begin an echo which will give East a count and enable him to hold off.

On the King of diamonds East plays the Ace, I the 4, and West the 9. East now leads the 6 of spades and dummy has to ruff with the 2 of hearts.

Let's see if I can count the hand. Probably West has seven spades and East a doubleton. West's 9 of diamonds could be a singleton, or it could be the beginning of an echo from a doubleton. I can't tell about the clubs. As to the hearts, I imagine that East has all five. If his only values had been a couple of tricks in diamonds he would probably have passed five diamonds. Players who double in such circumstances usually have even better defence against the first suit named. Moreover, this play of a spade to force the dummy is also suggestive of long trumps.

I can't draw his trumps by straight leads but I can exert some pressure by leading the 9 and forcing him to cover. That will leave me with a major tenace of sorts. So I lead the 9 of hearts from table, East plays the 10, I win with the King and West, as expected, shows out.

It looks as though East's distribution is two spades, five hearts, and either three diamonds and three clubs or four diamonds and two clubs. If he has three diamonds I think I can do it. My trumps are K J 6 3 with the Queen in dummy. East has the 8 7 5 4.

I play my second diamond to dummy, West playing the 5. I ruff a third diamond with my 3 of hearts, East playing the Jack, and take two rounds of clubs, finishing in dummy. Now I know the cards exactly, so I can show all four hands:

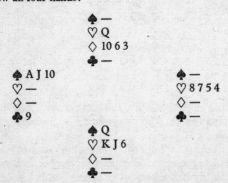

On the lead of a diamond from dummy East is caught in the diagonal crossfire of my trumps. Shaking his head, he plays the 7. I overruff,

ruff my spade with the Queen of hearts and win the last two tricks with the Jack and 6 of hearts, just making the contract.

This was the full deal:

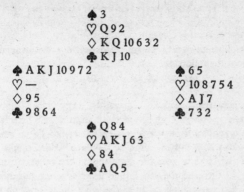

```
                    ♠ 3
                    ♡ Q 9 2
                    ◇ K Q 10 6 3 2
                    ♣ K J 10
♠ A K J 10 9 7 2                      ♠ 6 5
♡ —                                   ♡ 10 8 7 5 4
◇ 9 5                                 ◇ A J 7
♣ 9 8 6 4                             ♣ 7 3 2
                    ♠ Q 8 4
                    ♡ A K J 6 3
                    ◇ 8 4
                    ♣ A Q 5
```

Post-mortem

Looking at the full diagram I see that it would not have helped East to hold off the first diamond. In fact, there is no defence. The play shows the enormous power that can be exerted in an end-game when there are high trumps in both hands. That struck me some years ago when I constructed the following deal:

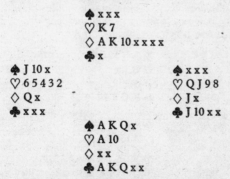

```
                    ♠ x x x
                    ♡ K 7
                    ◇ A K 10 x x x x
                    ♣ x
♠ J 10 x                              ♠ x x x
♡ 6 5 4 3 2                           ♡ Q J 9 8
◇ Q x                                 ◇ J x
♣ x x x                               ♣ J 10 x x
                    ♠ A K Q x
                    ♡ A 10
                    ◇ x x
                    ♣ A K Q x x
```

If you were by some odd chance to land in a contract of six hearts you could make it against any lead but a trump! You cash eight winners in the side suits and then lead a club from hand. Dummy's K 7 of hearts and your own A 10 will suffice to win four of the last five tricks.

13. A Profitless Overtrick

In a multiple team event, present opponents not the strongest in the field, I hold the following:

♠ 95 ♡ A K J 8 6 2 ◊ K 7 5 3 ♣ 4

The enemy are vulnerable, we are not. My partner, North, deals and opens **one spade**. East passes and I respond **two hearts**. Partner rebids **two spades**. I have two possible calls now. Three hearts is the more obvious one, but on some hands three spades might turn out better. If the bidding goes the same way at the other table South is likely to bid three hearts, and I think I'll play along with him. Three hearts in this sequence is fairly encouraging, so there is no reason to jump to four. I bid **three hearts**, therefore, and all pass. The bidding has been:

South	West	North	East
—	—	1♣	pass
2♡	pass	2♠	pass
3♡	pass	pass	pass

West leads the Queen of diamonds, and muttering something about a second suit partner puts down:

```
                    ♠ A Q 10 8 4
                    ♡ Q
                    ◊ 4 2
                    ♣ K Q 9 5 3
        ◊ Q led
                    ♠ 9 5
                    ♡ A K J 8 6 2
                    ◊ K 7 5 3
                    ♣ 4
```

With the Ace of diamonds on the right side, it looks as though we have underbid this. I play low from dummy; East puts on the Ace and returns a trump, which I run to dummy's Queen.

I would like to lead up to dummy's clubs but I don't feel disposed to take out my King of diamonds at this stage. If I do that I shall make nine tricks at most, for when they take the Ace of clubs they will cash a couple of diamonds. Though it may cost a trick in the suit I lead the King of clubs from dummy. East plays the 8 and West wins with the Ace. West returns the 6 of clubs; slightly unexpected, but not unwelcome. Trusting that it will not be ruffed, I put up the Queen. East drops the Jack and I discard a diamond. I come to hand by ruffing a club and on this trick East discards the 3 of spades.

It takes four rounds to draw the trumps, for West turns up with 10 9 x x, East with a doubleton. On the third and fourth rounds East discards two more spades. The following cards are left:

♠ A Q 10
♡ —
♢ 4
♣ 9

♠ 9 5
♡ 8
♢ K 7
♣ —

It is time to do some reconstruction. West appears to have had four hearts and five clubs. What has he got in spades and diamonds? He must have at least two diamonds and probably more. Odd that he didn't play a spade when he was in with the Ace of clubs! He may have a singleton King but hardly a low singleton, for that he would surely have led at some point. And East has thrown three spades, which is rather significant. In fact, I am beginning to think that the spades are 6 – 0.

If I lead a spade in the diagram position and West shows out, East will win and return a diamond. Then I shall have to lose another trick. But suppose I play off my last trump now? That may embarrass East and in any case it will be safe to finesse a spade afterwards, for East has no more clubs. On the 8 of hearts West throws a club, North a club, and East, after some reflection, the 6 of diamonds. Now I cash the King of diamonds, on which West plays the 9 and East the 10. At trick 11 a spade is led and West shows void. Dummy plays the 10, East the Jack, and a spade return in to the A Q gives me a diamond discard. Thus I end up with ten tricks. This was the full hand:

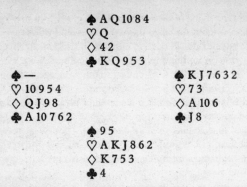

```
                    ♠ A Q 10 8 4
                    ♡ Q
                    ◇ 4 2
                    ♣ K Q 9 5 3
♠ —                                    ♠ K J 7 6 3 2
♡ 10 9 5 4                             ♡ 7 3
◇ Q J 9 8                              ◇ A 10 6
♣ A 10 7 6 2                           ♣ J 8
                    ♠ 9 5
                    ♡ A K J 8 6 2
                    ◇ K 7 5 3
                    ♣ 4
```

Making ten tricks at hearts against less than brilliant defence did not suffice to win the board, for at the other table the bidding went differently. North opened one club, East came in with one spade and South bid two hearts. Somewhat awkwardly placed for a rebid, North bid 2NT and South raised to 3NT. When East opened a spade declarer cashed the Queen of hearts and led a diamond, with the prospects of making about five tricks or nine, according to the position of the Ace of diamonds. His luck was in.

Post-mortem

This may seem a straightforward hand on which no one could go wrong, but the fact is that a declarer playing blind, in the sense of not thinking about the enemy hands, would play a spade after drawing trumps. He would not realize the advantage of playing off the last trump.

There was no defence to the end game, but it would have been better play for East, at trick 1, to let the Queen of diamonds run up to the King. That would have left the defence in better control. The contract would also have been held to nine tricks had West exited with a heart or a diamond when he was in with the Ace of clubs. The timing is different because the Queen of clubs has not been cashed.

14. The Diamonds were Paste

Playing rubber bridge against opponents of average standard, I pick up the following hand as South:

♠ Q 10 7 6 4 2   ♡ Q 10   ◇ J 5   ♣ Q 6 3

With no one vulnerable, West deals and passes. North opens **one club** and East overcalls with **one diamond**.

Some would say my hand wasn't good enough for a free bid but I don't hold with that. By passing you only create future problems. If the opponents jump the bidding, then on the next round you either have to pass again or come in at a high level. Besides, it's a fair hand, with a six-card major and the Queen of partner's suit. So, I call **one spade**.

After a pass by West, North bids **2NT** and East passes. I repeat my spades and after some thought partner gives me **four spades**. The bidding has gone:

South	West	North	East
—	pass	1♣	1◇
1♠	pass	2NT	pass
3♠	pass	4♠	pass
pass	pass		

West leads the 8 of diamonds and the dummy goes down:

```
                ♠ A K 5
                ♡ 9 7 4 2
                ◇ A Q 10
                ♣ A 10 4
◇ 8 led
                ♠ Q 10 7 6 4 2
                ♡ Q 10
                ◇ J 5
                ♣ Q 6 3
```

Wrong contract, I should think. We play a weak notrump not vulnerable. so North couldn't open 1NT, but with his strong diamonds

45

and good spades he might have preferred 3NT to four spades. Maybe I should have given him 3NT myself—I nearly did.

However, here we are in four spades and in danger of losing a diamond, two hearts and one or two clubs.

If they don't cash their two hearts at once I may get rid of a heart on the third diamond. At any rate, I'll take the slight risk of a ruff in diamonds and put up the Queen. Then if a low heart comes back West may play another diamond, thinking his partner has the K J.

East covers with the diamond King and leads back the 5 of hearts. I was expecting that, of course. I want to give an impression of strength in hearts, so I play the Queen. West wins with the King and returns the 3 of diamonds.

Thus far, my little deception has succeeded. After drawing trumps I can discard the 10 of hearts and the contract will depend on losing only one club. Before putting that suit to the test I want to find out as much about the hand as I can. I'd like to ruff a couple of hearts to get a count of that suit. I shall want entries to the table after drawing trumps, so I play the Queen of spades first (Of course, that is not the normal way to play such a combination, but is it impossible that East should have J 9 x x and West, who passed throughout, a void.)

Everyone follows to two rounds of spades, West showing up with J 9. After taking my discard on the third diamond I ruff a heart, East playing the 8, cross to dummy with the Ace of spades and ruff another heart, bringing down the Ace from East. Only four cards are left:

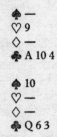

Let's see. West threw a club on the third diamond and another club on the third spade. I know that East started with six diamonds and two spades. Were his hearts A 8 5 or A J 8 5? I can't be certain, but in any event he has at most two clubs. Would he have overcalled on

♠ x x   ♡ A x x   ◇ K x x x x x   ♣ x x ?

It looks a bit naked, even not vulnerable. I think I'll assume that he has one of the honours. In that case, the play is Ace of clubs and a small club back, winning against K x or J x and losing only to x x.

Actually, East turns up with J x. The full hand was:

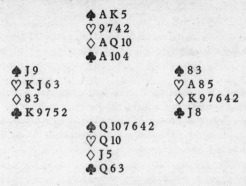

Post-mortem

There are quite a few points to note in the play:

The Queen of diamonds at trick 1, the best way to induce West to continue diamonds when next in.

The Queen of hearts at trick 2, to give an impression of strength in hearts, either A Q or K Q.

The use of entries to ruff hearts and obtain a fair count.

The play of the clubs. Observe that it would have been a losing play to finesse the 10. Had South been able to place East with a singleton club he would have played a low club from dummy at trick 10.

As to the defence, East knew the diamond position better than West and his return of a low heart was a slight error. He should have played Ace and another, to make sure that the defence took its heart tricks before declarer could obtain a discard on diamonds.

15. Avoiding Promotion

Playing in a game of rubber bridge of mixed quality, I deal and pick up one of my usual hands:

♠ Q763   ♡ 975   ◇ 72   ♣ J652

Both sides are vulnerable. I pass, West opens **one heart** and my partner **doubles**. East passes and I respond **one spade**. West bids **two diamonds** and partner jumps to **four spades**. I hope he knows what he's doing. West gives the matter some consideration but finally passes. The bidding has been:

South	West	North	East
pass	1♡	double	pass
1♠	2◇	4♠	pass
pass	pass		

West leads the King of diamonds and North puts down a good hand, though not quite so good as he thinks.

```
              ♠ K J 9 5
              ♡ A K
              ◇ A 10 4
              ♣ A Q 7 3
◇ K led
              ♠ Q 7 6 3
              ♡ 9 7 3
              ◇ 7 2
              ♣ J 6 5 2
```

There are only two certain losers but as West has bid two suits I can't rely on good breaks. For one thing, West may well have a singleton Ace of spades. For that reason I would prefer to lead the first round of spades from my own hand. I can come to hand only by ruffing a diamond, so I will hold off the first round.

West continues with the diamond Queen. I take the Ace and ruff the third round, East following suit throughout. I play a low spade, West plays low and the King of spades wins in dummy. Now if I lead a low spade back to the Queen West may play a fourth diamond and that may promote his partner's trump 10. Apart from that, I want an entry to my hand, so I play the Jack of spades from table. West takes this with the Ace and plays a low heart to dummy's King. The position is now:

♠ 9 5
♡ A
♢ —
♣ A Q 7 3

♠ Q
♡ 9 7
♢ —
♣ J 6 5 2

I have only lost two tricks but I am not too happy about the club situation. West bid two suits, has shown up with at least two spades and has not led a club at any point, as he might have done with a singleton. I don't think he has $2-5-4-2$ for he obviously thought about bidding over four spades. He could be $2-6-5-0$ or possibly $2-5-5-1$ and in that case the singleton club could well be the King.

If West is void in clubs I can make the contract all right by end-playing East. At the finish I can play a low club to the Jack and then return a club, ducking in dummy. But all that will be a mistake if West has the singleton King. Come to think of it, I can manoeuvre to play a third round of hearts and discover how that suit is distributed.

In the diagram position I play off the Ace of hearts, then draw the last trump, which is held by East. Now I play a heart and ruff with dummy's last spade. On this trick East discards the 4 of clubs.

Now it does look as though West is $2-6-5-0$ and East has all the clubs. I play a low club from table, East puts in the 8 and the Jack holds. Then I duck a club to East's 9 and win the last two tricks with dummy's A Q. This was the full hand:

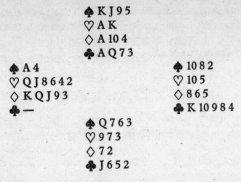

```
                    ♠ K J 9 5
                    ♡ A K
                    ◇ A 10 4
                    ♣ A Q 7 3
    ♠ A 4                              ♠ 10 8 2
    ♡ Q J 8 6 4 2                      ♡ 10 5
    ◇ K Q J 9 3                        ◇ 8 6 5
    ♣ —                                ♣ K 10 9 8 4
                    ♠ Q 7 6 3
                    ♡ 9 7 3
                    ◇ 7 2
                    ♣ J 6 5 2
```

Post-mortem

Note that it was advisable to play the first trump from hand in case West had a singleton Ace. Also, it would have been a mistake to lead a low trump from dummy on the second round, giving West a chance to promote the 10 in his partner's hand. As the hand developed it became clear that West was short in clubs. If he had held a low singleton he would probably have led it, but he might be void or he might have the singleton King.

Towards the end, declarer wanted to count the clubs. That is why he played off the Ace of hearts when in dummy so that a third heart could be ruffed. Had East followed to that trick declarer would have read him for 3 – 3 – 3 – 4 distribution and would have laid down the Ace of clubs, expecting West's singleton to be the King.

16. Message in Time

Playing in a team-of-four match against expert opposition, I hold:

♠ J 7 6   ♡ A Q J 6 5   ◇ Q 8 2   ♣ Q 7

The opponents are vulnerable, we are not. My partner, North, deals and passes and East passes. At the score I think I can chance a third hand opening of **one heart,** which may keep them out of 3NT. West overcalls with **two clubs** and my partner bids **two hearts.** East bids **three clubs** and this is passed to my partner. I hope he has his eye on the score and will allow for my having opened light third in hand. No, he bids **three hearts.** Both opponents give this consideration but neither doubles. So I end up as declarer in three hearts after the following bidding:

South	West	North	East
—	—	pass	pass
1♡	2♣	2♡	3♣
pass	pass	3♡	pass
pass	pass		

West leads the King of clubs and the following dummy goes down:

♠ A Q 10 3
♡ 9 7 4 2
◇ K J 6
♣ 9 5

♣ K led

♠ J 7 6
♡ A Q J 6 5
◇ Q 8 2
♣ Q 7

Yes, I see he had a bit in reserve when he bid only two hearts on the first round. It looks as though I can make it with one out of two finesses.

West begins with King and Ace of clubs, East playing the 3 and 6. West then switches to the 10 of diamonds. I want to find out where the Ace is, so I put in the Jack from dummy. East plays the Ace and returns a diamond.

The simple game is to take that in dummy and finesse the Queen of hearts. However, there is no point in doing that if the finesse is bound to be wrong. How can I find out who has the heart King? If East had both missing Kings in addition to the Ace of diamonds, he would have bid 2NT on the way around. If I test the spades first and find that East has the King of spades then West must have the King of hearts.

But if I take this diamond in hand and finesse the Queen of spades, is there any danger of my running into a diamond ruff? It is just possible that East has five diamonds. On the other hand, if the spade finesse is wrong then the heart finesse will be wrong and I shall also go down if I take the diamond in dummy and finesse the Queen of hearts. So I really don't have to worry about a possible ruff in diamonds. I decide to win with the Queen of diamonds and finesse the Queen of spades.

When I lead the 6 of spades West plays the 5, dummy the Queen and East the King. East plays a third diamond to dummy's King, everyone following. The position is now:

♠ A 10 3
♡ 9 7 4 2
♢ —
♣ —

♠ J 7
♡ A Q J 6 5
♢ —
♣ —

On the lead of the 2 of hearts from dummy East plays the 8. I am not going to pay any attention to that as it could easily be a false card from 10 8 x. I go up with the Ace of hearts and, happy sight! West drops the King. I had the message about the two Kings just in time.

This was the full hand:

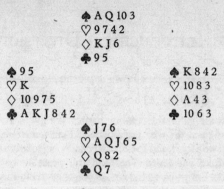

♠ A Q 10 3
♡ 9 7 4 2
♢ K J 6
♣ 9 5

♠ 9 5
♡ K
♢ 10 9 7 5
♣ A K J 8 4 2

♠ K 8 4 2
♡ 10 8 3
♢ A 4 3
♣ 10 6 3

♠ J 7 6
♡ A Q J 6 5
♢ Q 8 2
♣ Q 7

Post-mortem

East made an interesting point at the end of the play.

"If you had played your 9 of spades on the first round," he told his partner, "I would have known you had a doubleton and would have held up my King. Then declarer would have taken the finesse in hearts and you would have made your singleton King."

That is true. Also, if East had led a trump after the Ace of diamonds I would have had to finesse. From East's point of view, however, it was possible that his partner had Q 10 9 or Q 10 8 of diamonds and that the defence could establish a second diamond trick before the King of spades was forced out.

17. Introducing a Diversion

Playing rubber bridge against strong opponents, I hold the following:

♠ K 9 6   ♡ J 8 5 6   ◇ K J 8 2   ♣ A J

Both sides are vulnerable and my partner is the dealer. He opens
one diamond and the next player passes. I am too strong for three
diamonds, as we play it, and I'm certainly not going to make a scientific
approach bid of one heart. The hand will probably be played in
notrumps and I'm going to bid an old-fashioned 2NT. Partner raises
to 3NT and that is the end of a simple auction:

North	West	South	East
1◇	pass	2NT	pass
3NT	pass	pass	pass

West leads the 6 of clubs and partner goes down with this disappointing collection:

♠ A 8 4
♡ K 10 7
◇ A Q 9 6 3
♣ 8 3

♣ 6 led

♠ K 9 6
♡ J 8 6 5
◇ K J 8 2
♣ A J

Both short in clubs! That's annoying—not that we'd have much
chance of game in any other contract. On the first trick East plays the
Queen of clubs. It would be foolish to hold up and expose my weakness,
so I win with the Ace.

There are eight tricks on top but the clubs are wide open. What are
my chances of slipping through a heart, supposing that West has the
Ace? It would work against some players because West cannot tell that
my Jack of clubs is now single. But this West has played the game
before and he will be suspicious if I play on hearts instead of on

diamonds. He is quite good enough to go up with the Ace of hearts and lay down the King of clubs. It would be less suspicious if I played a couple of rounds of diamonds without showing that the suit was solid.

That must be the best plan. I lead the 8 of diamonds to dummy's Queen and return a low diamond to the King. On the second diamond West shows void, discarding a small spade. That's just as well. Having a singleton West may well conclude that his partner holds four to the Jack. Now I must try the heart. I lead the 5, West plays the 4 and dummy's King holds the trick.

That has passed off well. I have nine tricks now. When I play off the remaining diamonds West discards another low spade, the 9 of hearts and the 10 of spades. After the fifth diamond the following cards are left:

♠ A 8 4
♡ 10 7
♢ —
♣ 8

♠ K 9 6
♡ J 8
♢ —
♣ J

On the Ace of spades West drops the Queen. Goodness me, I'm going to make an overtrick. It must be completely safe to finesse the 9 of spades. And so it is, the full hand being:

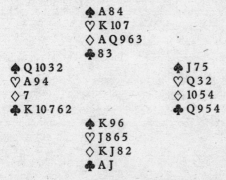

♠ A 8 4
♡ K 10 7
♢ A Q 9 6 3
♣ 8 3

♠ Q 10 3 2   ♠ J 7 5
♡ A 9 4   ♡ Q 3 2
♢ 7   ♢ 10 5 4
♣ K 10 7 6 2   ♣ Q 9 5 4

♠ K 9 6
♡ J 8 6 5
♢ K J 8 2
♣ A J

There are a number of points worth noting in this hand:

It would not be good play to hold up the Ace of clubs on the first trick, thus exposing the weakness in clubs.

It would be poor play to run off the five diamonds, giving the defence a chance to signal to one another and to realize that they have to win four club tricks.

If South plays a low heart at trick 2 an expert West might well go up with the Ace of hearts and lay down the King of clubs. From the failure to play on diamonds he would judge that declarer was trying to slip through a ninth trick.

That is why South had to introduce a diversion by playing the diamonds in a way that gave West the impression that his partner controlled the fourth round. The same sort of technique can be applied to almost all suit combinations when one of the high honours is held in the closed hand.

18. Full Stretch

Playing a team-of-four match against first-class opponents, I hold the following third in hand:

$$\spadesuit \text{Q} \quad \heartsuit \text{K Q 10 6 4 2} \quad \diamondsuit \text{A Q 9 6} \quad \clubsuit \text{J 7}$$

We are vulnerable and they not. After two passes I open **one heart** and West overcalls with **one spade**. Partner bids **1NT** and East **two spades**.

My hand is really not worth more than three hearts now, but at this vulnerability it is sound tactics to overbid a little. They are almost sure to sacrifice in four spades if I bid four hearts with confidence. Partner having bid 1NT freely, we should be able to beat four spades by a trick or two. So I jump to **four hearts**.

West, as expected, defends with **four spades** but partner now surprises me by going to **five hearts**. That is passed out, so the bidding has been:

South	West	North	East
—	—	pass	pass
1♡	1♠	1NT	2♠
4♡	4♠	5♡	pass
pass	pass		

West leads the 8 of diamonds and partner puts down:

$$\spadesuit \text{A 10 5}$$
$$\heartsuit \text{J 7}$$
$$\diamondsuit \text{J 4 3 2}$$
$$\clubsuit \text{A 10 5 3}$$

◇ 8 led

$$\spadesuit \text{Q}$$
$$\heartsuit \text{K Q 10 6 4 2}$$
$$\diamondsuit \text{A Q 9 6}$$
$$\clubsuit \text{J 7}$$

At total-point scoring North would no doubt have doubled four spades, taking the certain penalty. At the international match-point scoring that we use in these matches, to accept a penalty of 500 instea of making 650 means a loss of 4 I.M.P. Not knowing that my fou hearts was a bit of a push, partner has decided to play for the vulnerabl game instead of taking a penalty. For my part, I would rather b collecting a safe 500 or so from four spades doubled.

Now what are the prospects in five hearts? At least one club an one heart to lose. That diamond lead could be a singleton. They hav bid up to four spades on such moderate values, I'm sure West has singleton somewhere. If I am going to play on that assumption I mus cover with the Jack of diamonds to create a finesse position. East cover the Jack with the King and I win with the Ace.

Before I take any finesses in diamonds I have to draw trumps. I ma be short of entries to the table but I'll have to see what develops. O the 2 of hearts West plays the 5 and dummy's Jack holds the trick A heart is returned from the table and both follow, West winning wit the Ace. Perhaps West will simplify matters for me by leading a lo club or a low spade away from the King. Even a trump back won't d me any harm as I still have two entries left to dummy for diamond leads

These hopes are vain, for West plays the only card I didn't want t see—the King of spades. It won't help me to duck, because they won' play another spade into the A 10. I win with the Ace and this is th position:

♠ 10 5
♡ —
◇ 4 3 2
♣ A 10 5 3

♠ —
♡ K 10 6 4
◇ Q 9 6
♣ J 7

I can take a deep finesse in diamonds now, but there is still a trump out and West very likely has it. Is there any other chance worth con sidering? Maybe I can do something with the clubs. Since East has s far shown only the King of diamonds he must have at least one clu honour. In that case I think I can embarrass him in the end game. T begin with, I'm going to ruff a spade and draw the last trump.

West turns out to have the third trump, East discarding a spade Now I lead the Jack of clubs and West covers with the Queen. I pla the Ace from dummy and lead a low diamond, East following with the 5. Now have I any reason to change my original theory about the diamonds? West appears to have at least five spades headed by the K J, Ace of hearts and Queen of clubs. There is no certainty, but I think he is more likely to be 5 – 3 – 1 – 4 than 5 – 3 – 2 – 3.

Somewhat anxiously I put in the 6 of diamonds and it holds the trick. Now I am home, assuming that East has the King of clubs. I play off two more trumps, coming down to Q 9 of diamonds and 7 of clubs. At trick 11 I exit with a club and East has to play into my diamond tenace.

The full hand:

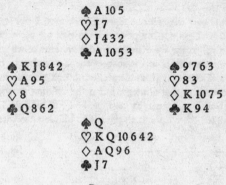

```
                    ♠ A 10 5
                    ♡ J 7
                    ◇ J 4 3 2
                    ♣ A 10 5 3
   ♠ K J 8 4 2                      ♠ 9 7 6 3
   ♡ A 9 5                          ♡ 8 3
   ◇ 8                              ◇ K 10 7 5
   ♣ Q 8 6 2                        ♣ K 9 4
                    ♠ Q
                    ♡ K Q 10 6 4 2
                    ◇ A Q 9 6
                    ♣ J 7
```

Post-mortem

West's lead of the singleton diamond was based on the hope that his partner would have a quick entry such as the Ace of spades. Most players would have done the same, but my experience is that singleton leads by the side that is weaker in high cards lose a trick much more often than they gain one. A frequent result, as on the present hand, is that a finesse position is created which the declarer could hardly have found for himself.

19. Reward for Sacrifice

Playing in a pairs event against moderate opposition, I hold:

♠ K 8　♡ 10 7 5 2　◇ Q J 10 8 6 3　♣ A

The opponents are vulnerable and we are not. East, on my right, deals and opens **one spade**. I overcall with **two diamonds** and West bids **two spades**. Partner raises to **three diamonds** and East jumps to **four spades**.

I have some sort of defence against four spades. I can lead my Ace of clubs and perhaps put my partner in to give me a club ruff. After that I might still make the King of spades or some other trick. If the opposition were strong I might suspect them of trying to bounce me into five diamonds at the vulnerability. I don't think my present opponents are up to that strategy, but if the bidding goes this way at other tables South will generally sacrifice. So I will bid **five diamonds**. This is **doubled** by West and all pass. The bidding has been:

South	West	North	East
—	—	—	1♠
2◇	2♠	3◇	4♠
5◇	double	pass	pass
pass			

Knowing that his side has the balance of the high cards, West opens the trump 5. That looks to me like a good lead for the defence when dummy goes down with the following:

```
              ♠ 6 3
              ♡ 8 3
              ◇ A K 9
              ♣ Q 10 9 6 4 2

◇ 5 led

              ♠ K 8
              ♡ 10 7 5 2
              ◇ Q J 10 8 6 3
              ♣ A
```

I win this trick with the King of diamonds and East follows with the 2. If the trumps are 3 – 1, which is likely, they may keep me from ruffing any hearts at all. If I make only eight tricks, losing four hearts and a spade, that will surely be bad. I wonder if I can do anything with the clubs. If East has K J alone I can, but that's rather a slender chance. Suppose he has something like K x x. I can lead a club to the Ace, return to the King of diamonds and lead the Queen of clubs. But that's no good, as I'm short of an entry to dummy.

I might try leading the Queen of clubs from dummy. Yes, that's worth considering. If East has the King he may cover, and that should save me a trick or two. If I am going to make that play I had better do it quickly, so I call for the Queen of clubs. East looks at this for a moment, then covers with the King. The Ace wins and West plays the 3. I enter dummy with a diamond, on which East discards a spade. (I'm glad to see that because if the diamonds had been 2 – 2 we would have had a sure defence against four spades.)

Now if East's clubs are the K J alone I can make the contract by leading a low club from dummy, but if he has K J x I have to lead the 10. I think that must be the better play for two reasons. East's slight hesitation before covering the Queen of clubs suggests that he had K J x rather than K J alone. Secondly, if I lead the 10 I shall set up a trick for the 9 whatever happens. That will save me from going more than two down.

When I lead the 10 of clubs from table East again looks worried. Finally he puts on the Jack. I ruff and enter dummy with a third round of trumps. When both opponents follow to the 9 of clubs I am able to discard all four hearts on this trick and the remaining clubs. The Ace of spades is right, so I finish up with a most unexpected overtrick.

East's play in covering the Queen of clubs made a difference of four tricks, as the full hand will show:

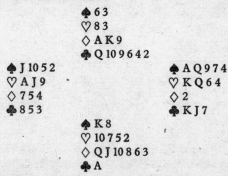

```
                    ♠ 6 3
                    ♡ 8 3
                    ◇ A K 9
                    ♣ Q 10 9 6 4 2
   ♠ J 10 5 2                          ♠ A Q 9 7 4
   ♡ A J 9                             ♡ K Q 6 4
   ◇ 7 5 4                             ◇ 2
   ♣ 8 5 3                             ♣ K J 7
                    ♠ K 8
                    ♡ 10 7 5 2
                    ◇ Q J 10 8 6 3
                    ♣ A
```

This type of play—the lead of the Queen of clubs towards the singleton Ace—is not exploited as much as it could be. The same sort of play can be made with J 9 8 x x x opposite a singleton Ace or J 9 8 x x opposite doubleton A K or A Q. There are many similar situations.

It was not so easy for the defence to judge the right play. If declarer had held A x in clubs he might have made the same play of the Queen from dummy and then it would have been fatal for East not to cover.

20. Second Choice

Playing with a lady partner in a mixed pairs event, I hold as dealer:

♠ A K Q 8 4 ♡ A Q J 10 6 ◇ — ♣ A 8 4

We are vulnerable, the opponents not. I am not sure whether to open two clubs, forcing to game in our system, or two spades, which shows a strong hand and is forcing for one round. The hand is good enough for two clubs but at this vulnerability I think it is better to name one of my suits on the first round. If I open with a conventional two clubs they may be able to pre-empt in diamonds before I have had a chance to show either suit, so I open **two spades**.

The opponents are silent and partner makes the negative response of **2NT**. To show my extra strength I jump to **four hearts**. Partner gives that some consideration and eventually bids **five spades**. That makes the bidding up to now:

South	West	North	East
2♠	pass	2NT	pass
4♡	pass	5♠	pass
?			

I wonder what she has! Something like King of hearts and J x x of spades, I should think, or perhaps a singleton heart and four spades. I'm certainly going six and I just wonder whether I can invite seven. At best she could have three spades, King of hearts and King of clubs, but even then the third round of clubs is unaccounted for. I must be content with **six spades**. That makes the complete auction:

South	West	North	East
2♠	pass	2NT	pass
4♡	pass	5♠	pass
6♠	pass	pass	pass

West leads the Queen of diamonds and I observe that we are quite high enough when partner puts down:

                    ♠ 7 5 2
                    ♡ K
                    ♢ K 9 7 6 3
                    ♣ J 9 7 3

    ♢ Q led

                    ♠ A K Q 8 4
                    ♡ A Q J 10 6
                    ♢ —
                    ♣ A 8 4

Assuming that the spades break, I can see eleven tricks on top. Somehow I've got to negotiate a club ruff. Before thinking it out I'll see what happens to the first trick.

Is there any possibility that West has underled the Ace of diamonds? Not really, and the King of diamonds may come in useful if the hand breaks badly. So I play a low diamond from dummy, East plays the 5 and I ruff with the 4 of spades.

Now I could play a heart to the King, draw two rounds of trumps and discard three clubs from dummy on A Q J of hearts. If no one ruffed I could then trump a club and make my twelfth trick that way. For that play to succeed the spades have to be 3 – 2, the hearts 4 – 3, and the hand with four hearts must have the three trumps. Not very promising, but for the moment I don't see anything better.

At the second trick I lead the 6 of hearts to dummy's King. I come back to hand with the Ace of spades and lead the Ace of hearts, discarding a club from dummy.

Suddenly something strikes me. Instead of trying to throw three clubs from table on the high hearts, can't I duck a round of clubs and then discard only twice from the table?

That's a better line, surely. Instead of needing to find the same opponent with three spades and four hearts, I shall want the clubs to be 3 – 3 or, if they are 4 – 2, the same player to have four clubs and three spades. But I mustn't play off two rounds of trumps immediately, as then they may play a third trump when I duck the club. Also, I mustn't play off a third heart too soon because they might lead a fourth heart and bring about a trump promotion.

I shall duck the club immediately. On the lead of a low club from hand West plays the 2, dummy the 9 and East the 10. East plays a trump and all follow. The position is now:

♠ 7
♡ —
◇ K 9 7 6
♣ J 7

♠ Q 8
♡ Q J 10
◇ —
♣ A 8

All follow to a third round of hearts, dummy discarding a club. When I play the Ace of clubs and ruff a club the clubs turn out to be 3 – 3. I come back to hand by ruffing a diamond, draw the last trump and make the remaining hearts.

This was the full deal:

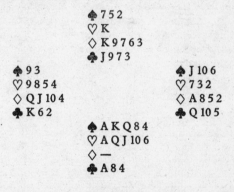

♠ 7 5 2
♡ K
◇ K 9 7 6 3
♣ J 9 7 3

♠ 9 3
♡ 9 8 5 4
◇ Q J 10 4
♣ K 6 2

♠ J 10 6
♡ 7 3 2
◇ A 8 5 2
♣ Q 10 5

♠ A K Q 8 4
♡ A Q J 10 6
◇ —
♣ A 8 4

Post-mortem

The line of play that I first thought of would have been no good. If I had drawn two trumps and tried to discard three clubs on the high hearts, East would have ruffed the fourth round of hearts, leaving me a trick short.

The play of ducking a club early is for some reason not easy to see. Most players, when shown the hand, tend to miss it.

The deal also presents an interesting defensive point. If West happens to lead the 2 of clubs originally and East plays the 10 declarer ducks with the same result. But suppose East puts in the Queen? Then declarer will surely win with the Ace and rely on a finesse of the 9 of clubs for his twelfth trick.

That's one to remember!

21. Two Doubtful Doubles

Playing in a team event with a reliable partner, I hold:

♠ 4   ♡ A K J 8 4   ♢ A 8 6   ♣ K Q J 3

Neither side is vulnerable and I am fourth in hand. After two passes East, on my right, opens **one diamond**.

This is a familiar situation in which there is no good bid. The objection to a double is that partner will probably respond in spades. A jump overcall of two hearts would be strength-showing in my system but would suggest more of a one-suited hand. Some players would favour a simple one heart on the grounds that this would be more likely to attract further bidding than a higher call.

In my opinion the disadvantage of a double in this sort of situation is usually exaggerated. If partner does bid spades the roof won't fall down. I can bid two hearts over one spade and consider the matter again over two spades. At any rate I decide to **double** and see what happens.

West passes and partner makes the strength-showing response of **two diamonds**. I didn't expect that. We play that response in the enemy suit as forcing for at least two rounds, so when East passes I simply bid **two hearts**.

Another surprise! Partner raises to **four hearts**. That makes the bidding to date:

South	West	North	East
—	pass	pass	1◇
double	pass	2◇	pass
2♡	pass	4♡	pass
?			

He can't have less than one Ace and a singleton diamond or equivalent values. A small slam looks certain. What about a grand? East opened third in hand and may be psychic. It is possible for partner to have two Aces, second-round control of diamonds and Queen of hearts. I think I'll bid 4NT and if he responds five hearts (showing two Aces) I will make a grand slam suggestion by bidding six diamonds.

In response to **4NT** partner bids **five diamonds**. Well, I must settle for **six hearts. Double,** says West. Perhaps I have done the wrong thing. We shall see.

The full bidding:

South	West	North	East
—	pass	pass	1◇
double	pass	2◇	pass
2♡	pass	4♡	pass
4NT	pass	5◇	pass
6♡	double	pass	pass
pass			

West leads the 2 of diamonds and partner displays the following:

♠ A Q 9 8
♡ Q 10 9 2
◇ K 10 4
♣ 10 8

◇ 2 led

♠ 4
♡ A K J 8 4
◇ A 8 6
♣ K Q J 3

The dummy is about what I expected.

So far as I can see, this is going to be a lay-down unless the hearts are 4 – 0. I play the 4 of diamonds on the first trick, East plays the 9 and I win with the Ace. I lay down the Ace of hearts and East discards a diamond. Disappointing but not surprising.

There are eleven tricks on top—five hearts, three clubs, two diamonds and one spade. The spade finesse would make twelve. What about a squeeze if East has the King of spades and the long diamonds? Can I manoeuvre an ending in which my last two cards are a spade and a diamond while dummy has the A Q of spades?

No, I can see two objections to that plan. West must have one of the high cards, probably the Ace of clubs, and when he comes in he will lead a spade through the dummy. Furthermore, even if East had the Ace of clubs, he could hold it up for one round and put me back in dummy, so that's no good.

I'd like to discover who has the Ace of clubs, but if I play a club early on I shall be exposed to a ruff should East have the Ace of clubs and

West a singleton diamond. But there's West's double to be accounted for. He wouldn't double a slam on the strength of his partner's third-hand opening unless he had at least one sure trick. I'm definitely inclined to place him with the Ace of clubs. If so, I wonder whether I can throw two diamonds from dummy on my good clubs and then play some sort of cross-ruff. I must examine that. If West follows to four rounds of clubs that play can't go wrong.

If I am going to play for this cross-ruff I don't want to draw any more trumps now. I am going to put these clubs to the test. I play the 3 of clubs to dummy's 10, which holds. A club is led back and West wins with the Ace. After studying the position West leads the 6 of spades. I win this in dummy and the position is then as follows:

♠ Q 9 8
♡ Q 10 9
◇ K 10
♣ —

♠ —
♡ K J 8 4
◇ 8 6
♣ K J

I ruff a spade and lead the King of clubs, throwing a diamond from dummy. When West follows to the Jack of clubs I discard another diamond and make the rest of the tricks by a cross-ruff.

The full hand turns out to be:

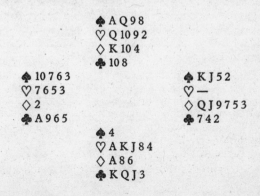

♠ A Q 9 8
♡ Q 10 9 2
◇ K 10 4
♣ 10 8

♠ 10 7 6 3   ♠ K J 5 2
♡ 7 6 5 3   ♡ —
◇ 2   ◇ Q J 9 7 5 3
♣ A 9 6 5   ♣ 7 4 2

♠ 4
♡ A K J 8 4
◇ A 8 6
♣ K Q J 3

Post-mortem

It seemed during the play that it was essential that West should follow to four rounds of clubs. Actually that is not so, for if West had had a club less and a spade more it would have been possible to ruff out East's King of spades.

One lesson from the hand is the old one that it does not pay to double slam contracts when the double can give any information. This contract would surely have failed had declarer not been able to place West with the Ace of clubs.

22. Counted Out

In a game of rubber bridge against resourceful opponents I deal myself the following:

♠ Q 7   ♡ A K 9 6 5   ◇ A Q J 2   ♣ Q 6

Both sides are vulnerable and I open **one heart**. The opponents are silent and my partner raises to **two hearts**. I may not make it but I must go to **four hearts**. That concludes a simple auction:

South	West	North	East
1♡	pass	2♡	pass
4♡	pass	pass	pass

West leads the King of clubs and with suitable apologies partner puts down:

♠ A 6 4
♡ J 10 8 4
◇ 7 6
♣ 9 5 4 3

♣ K led

♠ Q 7
♡ A K 9 6 5
◇ A Q J 2
♣ Q 6

East plays the 2 of clubs on the first lead and the 8 of clubs when West continues with the Ace. West then switches to the 2 of spades. He can hardly be leading away from the King but it costs me nothing to let it run. East, as expected, plays the King and returns the 3 of spades.

Now I have to find the diamond finesse right and not lose a trick in hearts. The diamond finesse may be right or wrong—there's nothing I can do about that. As to the hearts, I'd like to get a count of the hand if I can. If the hearts are 2 – 2 I won't need the Ace of spades as an entry and equally I can do without the discard. I overtake the Queen of spades with the Ace and finesse the Queen of diamonds.

The diamond finesse wins. I cash the Ace of hearts but nothing appears. Now I'd like to play the Ace of diamonds and ruff a diamond to get a further count, but I pause to consider if there is any danger in that. I don't think so. West appears to have four spades and four clubs, so if he's going to ruff a third round of diamonds it will be from Q x x in hearts.

All follow to the Ace of diamonds and on the 2 of diamonds West plays the 9, dummy ruffs and the King comes down from East. The position is now:

♠ 6
♡ J 10
◇ —
♣ 9 5

♠ —
♡ K 9 6 5
◇ J
♣ —

I think I have a complete picture now. Unless both opponents were false-carding in spades they are 4 – 4. As to the clubs, my original impression was that they were 4 – 3, but let me check that. West led the King and East played the 2. Then West continued with the Ace and East played the 8. West wouldn't have played a second round from A K x in case he were setting up the Queen. So that marks East with three clubs and, to judge from the fall of the King of diamonds, three diamonds. In short, he seems to be 4 – 3 – 3 – 3. If East plays low on the Jack of hearts I'm going to finesse.

Misery! West wins with the Queen of hearts and I am one down.

"Then you had five spades?" I say to East.

"No, only four," he answers. "But I've got another diamond tucked away somewhere."

Yes, he has fooled me, for this is the full hand:

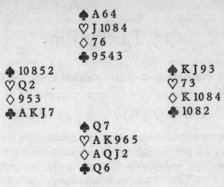

```
                    ♠ A 6 4
                    ♡ J 10 8 4
                    ♢ 7 6
                    ♣ 9 5 4 3
    ♠ 10 8 5 2                    ♠ K J 9 3
    ♡ Q 2                         ♡ 7 3
    ♢ 9 5 3                       ♢ K 10 8 4
    ♣ A K J 7                     ♣ 10 8 2
                    ♠ Q 7
                    ♡ A K 9 6 5
                    ♢ A Q J 2
                    ♣ Q 6
```

Post-mortem

All one can say of this hand is that it is a mistake to underestimate one's opponent's. The declarer's manoeuvres to obtain a count were sound enough in themselves but were easily read by the defence. In this company no reliance should have been placed on the fall of the King of diamonds.

23. Lucky Pin

In a rubber bridge game of average standard I hold the following in last position:

♠965 ♡AKJ84 ◇KJ8 ♣A10

West, on my left, deals and opens **one spade**. This is followed by two passes. I am too strong for a simple overcall of two hearts in the protective position, so I **double**. West passes and my partner responds **two clubs**. Now I introduce **two hearts** and partner raises to **three hearts**. My three small spades are unattractive but I don't like to languish in three when there is a fair chance of a vulnerable game. I bid **four hearts** and all pass. The bidding has been:

South	West	North	East
—	1♠	pass	pass
double	pass	2♣	pass
2♡	pass	3♡	pass
4♡	pass	pass	pass

West opens the King of spades and partner puts down:

♠832
♡Q102
◇A52
♣K753

♠ K led

♠965
♡AKJ84
◇KJ8
♣A10

At first sight it looks as though I shall have to find the diamond finesse or perhaps squeeze West should he have four clubs and the Queen of diamonds. On the King of spades East plays the 7. West continues with the Ace, dropping his partner's Queen, then Jack of spades, on which East discards the 2 of clubs.

West exits with a trump and I draw three rounds. On the third round East discards the 4 of diamonds. The cards are now as follows:

♠ —
♡ —
♢ A 5 2
♣ K 7 5 3

♠ —
♡ K J
♢ K J 8
♣ A 10

Since West has turned up with five spades and three trumps any idea of squeezing him in diamonds and clubs is out as there is not room for him to have the guarded Queen of diamonds and four clubs. Unless he has opened semi-psychic he should have both the minor suit Queens. Could the Queen of diamonds be doubleton? To judge from the discarding, I think not. If East had held only four clubs he would not have let one go so early, seeing the four clubs on the table. I am certainly inclined to place East with four diamonds and five clubs.

If West has Q 9 x or Q 10 x of diamonds there is nothing I can do against best defence, though it is possible that if I were to lead the Jack he might not cover from Q 9 x. But if West has Q x x and East 10 9 x I may be able to bring some pressure to bear on East. At any rate it cannot lose at this point to lead a trump and discard the 2 of diamonds from dummy.

On this trick West discards a spade and East another diamond. It is obvious that East began with five clubs and cannot let another one go. I am going to lead the Jack of diamonds in the hope that his two remaining diamonds are the 10 9.

West plays low on the Jack of diamonds. Having taken this view of the diamonds I must let the Jack run. If it loses to the Queen I shall look foolish, not for the first or last time. But all is well. East plays the 9 and I make the rest of the tricks, the full hand being:

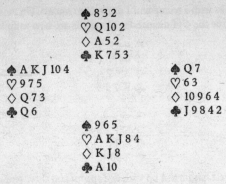

♠ 8 3 2
♥ Q 10 2
♦ A 5 2
♣ K 7 5 3

♠ A K J 10 4
♥ 9 7 5
♦ Q 7 3
♣ Q 6

♠ Q 7
♥ 6 3
♦ 10 9 6 4
♣ J 9 8 4 2

♠ 9 6 5
♥ A K J 8 4
♦ K J 8
♣ A 10

Post-mortem

Like most hands, this one was easy enough to play once declarer made the right inferences, all simple enough in themselves. When it became apparent that West had five spades and three hearts it followed that he could not be squeezed in clubs and diamonds.

The fact that East had discarded a club at the first opportunity was evidence that he had five. That meant that West could have only two clubs and therefore must have at least three diamonds. That these most likely included the Queen could be inferred from the fact that West had opened the bidding and East had passed the opening bid. (Remember that East had already turned up with the Queen of spades.) Thus it became clear that the only hope was to exert pressure on East in the minor suits.

To play such hands correctly it is not necessary to be a master of squeeze technique. The important thing, as always, is to keep alive to what is going on.

24. Major Road

Playing in a team event against strong opposition I pick up this powerful two-suiter:

♠ A K 7 6 4 2 ♡ A K J 8 5 3 ◇ A ♣ —

Both sides are vulnerable and I am first to speak. I like to make a start with my suits on this type of hand in preference to bidding an artificial two clubs, so I open **two spades**, forcing for one round in our system. If partner gives me a negative response I will jump to four hearts. On this occasion West overcalls with three diamonds, North passes and so does East. I jump to **four hearts**, as planned, but this does not silence West. He bids **five clubs**.

Now my partner supports to **five spades** and East bids **six clubs**. I could bid six diamonds now to suggest the possibility of a grand slam to my partner. However, I think I ought to be content to play this hand in six if they will let me. The suits are sure to break badly. So I am content with **six spades** and the opponents compete no further. This has been the adventurous auction:

South	West	North	East
2♠	3◇	pass	pass
4♡	5♣	5♠	6♣
6♠	pass	pass	pass

West opens the King of diamonds and I see that my partner's five spades was imaginative:

```
              ♠ J 10 5 3
              ♡ 10 6 2
              ◇ 5 4 2
              ♣ 6 4 3

◇ K led

              ♠ A K 7 6 4 2
              ♡ A K J 8 5 3
              ◇ A
              ♣ —
```

77

After winning the first trick with the Ace of diamonds I lay down the Ace of spades. West discards a diamond, which is sad but not surprising.

Now how am I going to encompass these major suits? I can give up a trick to the Queen of spades and then enter dummy with the Jack, but I am not yet sure whether or not I want to finesse in hearts. West could be 0 – 1 – 6 – 6 but I suppose he could also be 0 – 2 – 6 – 5.

Another way would be to give up a trick to the Queen of hearts and enter dummy with the 10 of hearts to take the marked finesse in spades. I can lay down Ace of hearts and then play the Jack. No, what am I thinking of? That will be all right if East has Q x x but calamitous if either defender has Q x.

Having formed two rather poor plans I now consider the possibility of leading the Jack of hearts first. That would lose only if West had Q x x in hearts. Then he would have to be 0 – 3 – 5 – 5 and East, with a singleton heart and four diamonds, would probably have raised the diamonds on the first round of bidding.

This hand is driving me mad. If West has Q x x in hearts I can't make the contract whatever I do. It is only if East has singleton Queen of hearts that the lead of the Jack will be a disaster.

At the end of these confused reflections I decide to lead the Jack of hearts. West stares at this card for some while, as well he may. Eventually he puts on the Queen of hearts and leads the Ace of clubs. I ruff, enter dummy with the 10 of hearts, both defenders following, and claim the remainder with the aid of the spade finesse. This was the full hand:

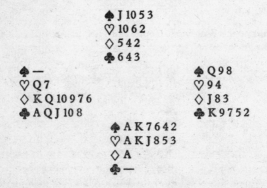

Post-mortem

The reader may well have been ahead of me on this hand. The lead of the Jack of hearts at trick 3 is obvious when one thinks of it, but I was very close to committing the folly of establishing entry to dummy in spades and finessing the Jack of hearts.

25. Proper Respect

Playing in a team-of-four match against capable opposition, I hold as dealer:

♠ Q 9   ♡ A 8 3   ♢ A K 10 9 4   ♣ J 9 7

Both sides are vulnerable and I open **one diamond**. West passes and my partner responds **one spade**. Having fair scattered values I rebid **1NT** rather than two diamonds. My partner raises to **3NT** and all pass. The bidding has been:

South	West	North	East
1♢	pass	1♠	pass
1NT	pass	3NT	pass
pass	pass		

West leads the 4 of clubs and this dummy goes down:

```
                    ♠ K 10 7 4 3
                    ♡ K 10 2
                    ♢ Q J 5
                    ♣ K 3

♣ 4 led

                    ♠ Q 9
                    ♡ A 8 3
                    ♢ A K 10 9 4
                    ♣ J 9 7
```

A club trick is certain after the lead, so there are eight tricks on top. A ninth can be established in spades but meanwhile they may set up four club tricks to accompany their Ace of spades. Well, I must play low from table and see what develops.

East plays the Ace of clubs on the first trick and returns the 6. When I play the 9 West puts on the 10 but I don't suppose that's from Q 10 x. More likely he has Q 10 x x x and is trying to convey to his partner that he controls the rest of the suit.

If the clubs are 4 – 4 (or 6 – 2, East having the Ace of spades) I am in no danger. The question is how to play if they are 5 – 3. I can run my diamonds and see what they discard or I can try to slip through a spade. Obviously I shan't be able to do that if West has the Ace of spades and three good clubs, but if East has the Ace of spades will he play it when I lead a low spade from table? I think so. He is quite a good player and, moreover, my failure to play diamonds would be suspicious. I am not going to insult him. I'll play off the diamonds and see if anything turns up.

West has to discard three times on the diamonds. He lets go, in order, 5 of hearts, 6 of spades and Jack of spades. East signals in spades, playing the 8 and then the 2. After the five diamonds the following cards are left:

$$\spadesuit \text{ K } 10 \text{ } 7$$
$$\heartsuit \text{ K } 10 \text{ } 2$$
$$\diamondsuit \text{ —}$$
$$\clubsuit \text{ —}$$

$$\spadesuit \text{ Q } 9$$
$$\heartsuit \text{ A } 8 \text{ } 3$$
$$\diamondsuit \text{ —}$$
$$\clubsuit \text{ J}$$

Neither player has discarded a club. That confirms my original impression that they were 5 – 3. So West has three clubs left and either three hearts or two hearts and a spade. If they are two hearts and a spade, I can do nothing (unless the hearts are Q J alone). But the Jack of spades may have been his last spade; maybe he couldn't let go another heart or thought he couldn't. I think I'll make the favourable assumption that he began with Q J x x in hearts and has been under pressure. I'd like to play off one round of hearts to see if the Queen or Jack falls, but if I do that I give up my tenace position. It's possible that he has discarded too well and has come down to Q J of hearts alone. But I'm going to play for what I think is the best chance and exit with the Jack of clubs.

West takes the Queen and plays off two more rounds of clubs. Since I can't afford to lose another trick and am hoping that West has no spade left I discard three spades from dummy and two from my own hand. That leaves me with K 10 2 of hearts on the table and A 8 3 in hand. At trick 11 West, as I was hoping, leads the 6 of hearts.

The only question now is whether that lead is from Q 9 x (or J 9 x) or from Q J x. I must assume from Q J x because with an original

holding of Q 9 x x or J 9 x x he could have let go another heart and
kept a spade. Also, he would exit now with the Queen (or Jack) and not
with a low card. When I play the 10 from dummy it holds the trick, so
I make the contract. The full hand:

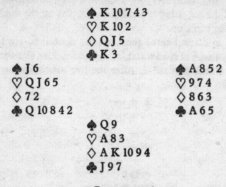

♠ K 10 7 4 3
♡ K 10 2
♢ Q J 5
♣ K 3

♠ J 6
♡ Q J 6 5
♢ 7 2
♣ Q 10 8 4 2

♠ A 8 5 2
♡ 9 7 4
♢ 8 6 3
♣ A 6 5

♠ Q 9
♡ A 8 3
♢ A K 10 9 4
♣ J 9 7

Post-mortem

The main point of this hand is to stress the advisability of playing
off the long suit. Players often underestimate the advantage of that
procedure. On a hand of this sort they say, "There can't be any squeeze
unless West has all the clubs and all the hearts plus the Ace of spades.
It must be a better chance to try to slip a round of spades past East."

Actually, as we saw, West was under pressure even though he did
not have the Ace of spades. A further practical consideration is that
defenders often make a mistake when a long suit is led against them.
Sometimes both players unguard the same suit; sometimes the player
with the long suit lets one go when he should not. It's not necessary
to see around corners. When there is no good alternative declarer
should play off his long suit even when there seems no likelihood of a
squeeze, pseudo or otherwise.

26. Lifeless Knave

Playing rubber bridge against opponents of average strength I deal and hold:

♠ A 10 9 8 6 4   ♡ Q 5   ◇ 8 6   ♣ A 10 4

As we are not vulnerable and they are, I make a light opening of **one spade**. West **doubles**, my partner **redoubles**, and East passes. The conventional way to indicate a limited hand with a long suit is to rebid the suit at this point, but as I am not sure whether my present partner will appreciate that, I decide to pass. West rescues himself into **two clubs**. This is passed by North and East. My partner expects me to say something, I know, and as I don't fancy a double of two clubs I bid **two spades**. Partner raises to **four spades** and all pass. The bidding has been:

South	West	North	East
1♠	double	redouble	pass
pass	2♣	pass	pass
2♠	pass	4♠	pass
pass	pass		

West leads the King of clubs. Remarking that he had hoped I would be able to double two clubs, partner puts down:

♠ K 3
♡ K 10 6 4 3
◇ A Q 10 2
♣ 8 7

♣ K led

♠ A 10 9 8 6 4
♡ Q 5
◇ 8 6
♣ A 10 4

Prospects seem reasonable. Assuming the diamond finesse to be right I should lose at most a spade, a heart and a club. On the first trick East plays the 2 of clubs and I let the King hold. West switches to the 5 of diamonds. I play dummy's Queen with fair confidence but East puts on the King. That's an unexpected blow!

Now I can't afford to lose a trump trick. I must assume West has a singleton spade and project the play on the assumption that the singleton is the Queen or Jack.

After the King of diamonds East returns the 7 of hearts to his partner's Ace and West exits with the 3 of diamonds. This second finesse is probably right, but the question is, will it help me at all?

Suppose that the 10 of diamonds holds. I can then throw a club on the Ace of diamonds and ruff a diamond. Now cash Ace of clubs, lead a spade to the King and finesse the 8 on the way back; overtake Queen of hearts, ruff a heart—and I'm still in the wrong hand at trick 12, unable to lead trumps through East.

This has got to be managed in a different way. If I'm going to play West for a singleton trump honour I need every possible entry to dummy, including the ruff of the third club. I think it can just be done. At any rate there is no point in finessing the diamond, so I go up with the Ace and ruff a diamond, East following suit. I overtake the Queen of hearts and ruff a heart. The hearts break 3 – 3 and this is now the situation:

```
        ♠ K 3
        ♡ 10 6
        ◇ 10
        ♣ 8

        ♠ A 10 9 8
        ♡ —
        ◇ —
        ♣ A 10
```

After cashing the Ace of clubs I ruff my last club with dummy's 3 and lead the 10 of diamonds. East, who is evidently down to four trumps, ruffs with the 2 of spades and I overruff with the 8. Now the 9 of spades brings the Queen from West. Dummy's King wins and I make the last two tricks with the A 10 over East's J 7, the full hand being:

```
            ♠ K 3
            ♡ K 10 6 4 3
            ◇ A Q 10 2
            ♣ 8 7
♠ Q                         ♠ J 7 5 2
♡ A J 8                     ♡ 9 7 2
◇ J 7 5 3                   ◇ K 9 4
♣ K Q J 5 3                 ♣ 9 6 2
            ♠ A 10 9 8 6 4
            ♡ Q 5
            ◇ 8 6
            ♣ A 10 4
```

Post-mortem

Dummy's singleton King of trumps opposite the A 10 9 8 proved a very powerful combination in the end-game. Note that the contract cannot be made if South uses dummy's 3 of spades for a finesse of the 8. The basic reason for this is that the small trump on the table is required as an extra entry. At the twelfth trick South picks up East's J 7 of spades by means of a trump coup.

27. Breaking Contact

Playing in a pairs event, with a high standard all round the table, I hold in fourth position:

♠ A Q 6   ♡ Q 8 4   ◇ Q 8 5   ♣ A Q 9 5

Neither side is vulnerable and West, on my left, opens one spade. This is followed by two passes. This is a situation I never care for. The natural action on my hand is to bid notrumps, but in this protective position there is such a wide gap between 1NT and 2NT. Players generally reopen with 1NT on about 11 to 14 points. Here I have 16 but I can hardly bid 2NT on it. Nor is it altogether satisfactory to double and then bid 2NT over a minimum response. Nevertheless, that is what I may have to do. For the moment, I **double**.

West passes and North bids **two diamonds**. East passes again. Technically I ought to pass now, but at match-point scoring I am not going to let him play in two diamonds. It's an overbid in a sense but I'm going to bid **2NT**. I only hope he doesn't take me too seriously and raise on about 5 or 6 points. No, all pass, so the bidding has been:

South	West	North	East
—	1♠	pass	pass
double	pass	pass	pass
2NT	pass	pass	pass

West leads the Jack of spades and partner puts down:

```
              ♠ 9 8 5 3
              ♡ 10 3 2
              ◇ J 9 7 2
              ♣ K 3

♠ J led

              ♠ A Q 6
              ♡ Q 8 4
              ◇ Q 8 5
              ♣ A Q 9 5
```

I wish I'd followed my instinct and reopened with 1NT on the

South hand. Next time I shall. It's not going to be easy to make 2NT but at least that's better than playing in two diamonds.

East plays the 2 of spades on the first trick and I win with the Queen. To make any tricks at all I've got to find the 10 of diamonds. It's more convenient to play West for that card than East, so to the second trick I lead the 5 of diamonds. West plays the 6 and I put in dummy's 7, which holds the trick. That's slightly better. I return the 2 of diamonds to the Queen and West wins with the King.

West now studies the matter at some length and finally exits with the 7 of spades. I put in the 8 from dummy and that holds the trick, East discarding the 2 of clubs. West has played a low spade because, from his point of view, I might have had A Q alone. Now I am on the table and this is the position:

                        ♠ 9 5
                        ♡ 10 3 2
                        ◇ J 9
                        ♣ K 3

                        ♠ A
                        ♡ Q 8 4
                        ◇ 8
                        ♣ A Q 9 5

The general lie of the cards is fairly plain. West began with K J 10 x x in spades and, according to all indications, A K 10 x in diamonds. He could have A x x in hearts and a singleton club or, perhaps more likely, A x in hearts and a doubleton club. I have made three tricks and can see four more but that is still one short. The trouble is that I cannot conveniently enjoy a second trick in diamonds. If I come to hand with the Ace of spades the defence will make too many tricks, and if I play a club to the Queen in order to lead a diamond the clubs will be blocked.

I wonder whether I can make a fourth trick out of the clubs. If West has something like J x or 10 x, which is not unlikely, I can establish a major tenace over East. But can I throw him in?

Now I think I'm getting somewhere. If West has a doubleton A x or K x of hearts I may be able to cut the communications between the defending hands and eventually throw East in on the third round of hearts. To do that I have got to find West with only one entry in hearts (for otherwise he will get his spades going). I can't do it if he has A J. But he may have A 9 and to take care of that I must lead the 10 from

87

dummy. On the 10 of hearts East plays the Jack, I play low and West follows with the 6. East exits with a heart to his partner's Ace. The hand is developing favourably, for West cannot cash his high diamond while I still have a club entry to table. West therefore exits with a spade to the Ace, and on this trick East has to throw a heart in order to keep his clubs. Now there are six cards left:

♠ 9
♡ 3
◇ J 9
♣ K 3

♠ —
♡ Q
◇ 8
♣ A Q 9 5

Prospects have improved but there is still a view to take in clubs. I play a club to the King, West following with the 6, and return a club on which East plays the 7. Now if East began with J 10 x x x I have to finesse the 9. However, he would then have been close to a response to the opening bid of one spade. Apart from that, I cannot resist the more artistic ending. So I put in the Queen, West drops the Jack and now I have them for sure! I exit with the Queen of hearts and after making two heart tricks East has to lead a club into my A 9.

This was the full deal:

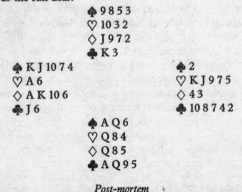

♠ 9 8 5 3
♡ 10 3 2
◇ J 9 7 2
♣ K 3

♠ K J 10 7 4
♡ A 6
◇ A K 10 6
♣ J 6

♠ 2
♡ K J 9 7 5
◇ 4 3
♣ 10 8 7 4 2

♠ A Q 6
♡ Q 8 4
◇ Q 8 5
♣ A Q 9 5

Post-mortem

While East was making his heart tricks at the finish West was sitting with two good spades and the Ace of diamonds. The two rounds of hearts had put the defending hands out of touch with one another.

The same sort of result can sometimes be effected by a deceptive play in a position such as the following:

$$\Diamond\ 9\ 7\ 3$$

$$\Diamond\ A\ Q\ J\ 10\ 4 \qquad\qquad \Diamond\ K$$

$$\Diamond\ 8\ 6\ 5\ 2$$

Playing either in a suit or at notrumps, South knows that West, although he has not led diamonds, has a five-card suit. Obviously if East gains the lead at any point he will lead his King and West will overtake. If West has no side entry, however, a low diamond from hand may trick him into playing the 10 and so losing contact with his partner.

28. Ground Level

My partner on this hand at rubber bridge is a good player and the opponents are of average strength. In fourth position I hold:

♠ Q 5 3 2　♡ A Q J 6 5 2　◇ 7　♣ A 6

Neither side is vulnerable and West opens **one club**. My partner passes and East raises to **two clubs**. I come in with **two hearts** and West passes. My partner raises to **three hearts**. I haven't much to spare after coming in at the range of two but game may be on if there is a reasonable fit in spades. I advance to **four hearts** and all pass. The bidding has been:

South	West	North	East
—	1♣	pass	2♣
2♡	pass	3♡	pass
4♡	pass	pass	pass

West opens the King of clubs and I see that partner also has been pressing a little:

```
              ♠ K 10 6
              ♡ 9 7 3
              ◇ A J 5 2
              ♣ 7 4 2

    ♣ K led
              ♠ Q 5 3 2
              ♡ A Q J 6 5 2
              ◇ 7
              ♣ A 6
```

The contract is going to depend on a number of factors—the finesses in the major suits and the break in spades. I have to consider whether or not to win the first club and whether to finesse the 10 of spades early or to cross to dummy and finesse the trumps first.

If the heart finesse is wrong I'll need three spade tricks, but if it's right I can afford to lose two spade tricks. That may have some bearing on how I play the suit, so I'm inclined to think I should settle the heart position before I play on spades.

Now can it make any difference whether or not I take the Ace of clubs at once? I don't really want an early switch to spades, threatening a ruff and making it dangerous to finesse in trumps. Taking the Ace at once will establish an entry for East, but that is unlikely to matter.

So I take the Ace of clubs, cross to the Ace of diamonds and finesse the Queen of hearts. This holds, West dropping the 10. I don't think it's likely that he is holding off from K 10 x—he is not that sort of player. The question now is how to tackle the spades on the assumption that the heart finesse is right. I don't want to finesse the 10 of spades, lose to the Jack and run into a spade ruff. If West's 10 of hearts is a singleton the spades are probably 4 – 2. As the clubs were supported and no one mentioned diamonds, West's most likely distribution is 4 – 1 – 4 – 4.

Now suppose West has A J x x in spades. I don't need to finesse the 10. If I lead low to the King, draw trumps and then lead a low spade towards the 10 6, that will be good enough. Of course East may have J x, but I can think about that later.

For the moment I'm going to play a low spade to dummy's King. That wins and I return a trump. (A spade would not be safe because if West had A J x left he would make the Jack and Ace and give his partner a ruff.) The second heart finesse wins, West discarding a club. On the Ace of hearts West discards a diamond. The following cards are left:

♠ 10 6
♡ —
♢ J 5 2
♣ 7 4

♠ Q 5 3
♡ 6 5 2
♢ —
♣ 6

I lead a low spade towards the dummy and West plays the 7. Now I'm sure the spades are 4 – 2, but if West had A J 7 x wouldn't he at any rate consider going up with the Jack in front of dummy's 10 x? It might not be right play but he would still think about it. I'm fairly confident that East has the bare Jack left. I'm going to stay close to the ground and play the 6 from dummy.

That turns out to be right, for East plays the Jack. That leaves the Queen and 10 of spades equals against West's Ace and I make the contract, having lost a club and two spades. The full hand was as follows:

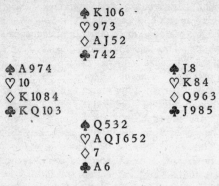

♠ K 10 6
♡ 9 7 3
◇ A J 5 2
♣ 7 4 2

♠ A 9 7 4
♡ 10
◇ K 10 8 4
♣ K Q 10 3

♠ J 8
♡ K 8 4
◇ Q 9 6 3
♣ J 9 8 5

♠ Q 5 3 2
♡ A Q J 6 5 2
◇ 7
♣ A 6

Post-mortem

Whenever a hand seems to call for two or more finesses it's important to decide on the priority. Sometimes one successful finesse will obviate the other, but not vice versa. In this hand the first play had to be the trump finesse because the management of the spades was going to depend to some extent on whether the heart finesse succeeded.

When West's 10 of hearts fell on the first round his distribution could be assessed with fair certainty. The clubs were likely to be 4 – 4 since they had been supported. The diamonds were sure to be 4 – 4 since neither defender had mentioned them. The 10 of hearts appeared to be a singleton, so West was marked with four spades.

Having reached that conclusion, South had to appreciate that it was not necessary to finesse the 10 of spades before drawing trumps. If West had A J x x it would be safe to win with the King and later lead towards the 10 x.

The next point was the psychological one that when West played the 7 of spades in front of dummy's 10 x it was unlikely that he had the A J. However, it is interesting to reflect that if West had in fact held something like A J 9 x it would have been a brilliant defence to play the 9 when declarer led low towards the table.

29. "Flight Square"

Playing a team-of-four match against opponents of average strength, I hold as dealer:

♠ A Q 10 9 6 4   ♡ 8 2   ◇ 9 7   ♣ A J 4

Neither side is vulnerable and I open **one spade**. West passes and my partner responds **two diamonds**. East comes in with **two hearts**. Although I have a minimum opening in terms of high cards I am not going to be deterred from rebidding my good suit, so I say **two spades**.

My partner now bids their suit, **three hearts**. I take this to mean that he has a control in hearts and is looking for game in either spades or notrumps. Having a fair guard in clubs I could bid 3NT, but my spades are broken and I have no high card in his suit. I think that **three spades** is more prudent. This he raises to **four spades** and all pass. The bidding has been:

South	West	North	East
1♠	pass	2◇	2♡
2♠	pass	3♡	pass
3♠	pass	4♠	pass
pass	pass		

West leads the King of hearts and I see that partner had in fact a difficult bid over two spades, his hand being:

```
            ♠ 7 3
            ♡ A 10
            ◇ A K 10 6 5 4 2
            ♣ Q 9
♡ K led
            ♠ A Q 10 9 6 4
            ♡ 8 2
            ◇ 9 7
            ♣ A J 4
```

I dare say we are as well off in four spades as 3NT, which would be an anxious affair after a heart lead.

As most players lead low from K x x this lead of the King may be
from a doubleton. I am going to duck and if they switch to diamonds
I can study the position again. East plays the 7 and West continues
with another heart, taking out dummy's Ace.

I can't rely on the diamonds breaking, especially as there was an
intervening bid. I must test the clubs, as I may want to ruff the third
round. East covers the Queen with the King. I cash the Ace and Jack
and when I ruff a third round with dummy's 7 I get my first surprise.
East throws a spade. That leaves the cards as follows:

♠ 3
♡ —
◇ A K 10 6 5 4 2
♣ —

♠ A Q 10 9 6 4
♡ —
◇ 9 7
♣ —

I have only lost one trick but I'm not all that happy about the hand.
Unless East is playing a remarkably deep game he couldn't overruff
the 7. That means that West has K J 8 in trumps, but what if he has
K J 8 x? I'll lose the second round to the King and West will put me
back on the table with a diamond. Then how can I get back to draw
trumps without promoting another trick for him?

Let me see if I can count the hand. West has six clubs, I know, and
probably a doubleton heart. If he has three spades the contract is safe
anyway, for I'll lose only two trump tricks. But if West has four spades?
Then he will have only one diamond and that's the situation I have to
guard against. I must play off a top diamond so that West can't put me
back on the table and promote an extra trump trick for himself.

All follow to the Ace of diamonds. Then I play Ace and Queen of
spades. East shows void on the second round. West is in with the
King but he hasn't got a diamond to play. He makes the Jack of
trumps in due course but that is all.

So I am just home in four spades. Three no trumps wouldn't have been a success, as the full hand shows:

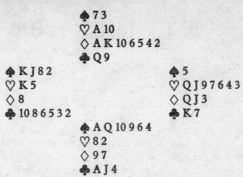

```
                    ♠ 7 3
                    ♡ A 10
                    ◇ A K 10 6 5 4 2
                    ♣ Q 9
    ♠ K J 8 2                      ♠ 5
    ♡ K 5                          ♡ Q J 9 7 6 4 3
    ◇ 8                            ◇ Q J 3
    ♣ 10 8 6 5 3 2                 ♣ K 7
                    ♠ A Q 10 9 6 4
                    ♡ 8 2
                    ◇ 9 7
                    ♣ A J 4
```

One must give credit to West for not doubling four spades.

Post-mortem

The play of the Ace of diamonds removed West's flight square, as the chess players call it. The play was by no means obvious because the count of West's hand was hypothetical, not inferential. There was danger only if West had four spades and the picture of the hand had to be built up on that premise.

30. The Light was Bad

Playing rubber bridge against old rivals I hold the following in second position:

♠ 9 3   ♡ A J   ◇ K 9 7 2   ♣ A J 10 8 6

Neither side is vulnerable and East, on my right, opens **one spade**. I can't very well make a take-out double on minimum values with a doubleton in the other major. It's not a particularly good overcall at the two level either, but I'm going to chance **two clubs**. West passes and my partner, a scientific player, bids **two spades**. Players seem to bid the enemy suit all the time nowadays with a variety of meanings. For the moment I don't see what I can do but bid **three clubs**. Partner raises that to **four clubs**. I don't know what he's playing at, but I'm going **five clubs**. All pass, so the bidding has been:

South	West	North	East
—	—	—	1♠
2♣	pass	2♠	pass
3♣	pass	4♣	pass
5♣	pass	pass	pass

West leads the 5 of spades and I see that we are in the wrong contract when this dummy goes down:

```
              ♠ 7 6 4 2
              ♡ 8 2
              ◇ A Q 6 3
              ♣ K Q 2

♣ 5 led

              ♠ 9 3
              ♡ A J
              ◇ K 9 7 2
              ♣ A J 10 8 6
```

On this lead of a low spade I should think the spades are 4 – 3 and that we could have made 3NT. That's not easy to bid, but five diamonds is a lay-down if the diamonds are 3 – 2. I suppose he'll tell me that I should have introduced diamonds on K x x x.

I don't see how I'm going to make five clubs unless they give me a chance to develop a squeeze in the major suits and that's not at all likely. East wins the first trick with the King of spades and continues with the Ace on which his partner plays the 8. East then switches to the King of hearts. That's what I was afraid of; now there's no chance of a genuine squeeze.

Nevertheless I see a chance of putting East to the test. When I have ruffed a third round of spades he will have the master spade left and the master heart. If I come down to a spade and a diamond on the table at trick 12 and lead the diamond, East may not be sure which card to keep. I can manipulate the diamonds with a certain amount of cunning so that he won't be sure, unless he has been watching very carefully, whether the diamond on the table is a master or not.

To bring about the position I want, I have to conceal the 2 of diamonds. After three rounds of trumps I ruff the third spade in hand, lead the 7 of diamonds to the Queen and return the 6 to the King. I play off my last trump, discarding a heart, and play the 9 of diamonds to the Ace. For once it is appropriate to set out a two-card ending:

♠ 7
♡ —
♢ 3
♣ —

♠ —
♡ J
♢ 2
♣ —

East's last two cards are the Jack of spades and the Queen of hearts. When I lead the 3 of diamonds from the table East sits up. I can hear his brain working: "That's not the last diamond, is it? No, South still has one." After a short pause East throws his spade and the last trick is won by dummy's 7 of spades. This is the full hand:

```
                    ♠ 7 6 4 2
                    ♡ 8 2
                    ◇ A Q 6 3
                    ♣ K Q 2
    ♠ Q 8 5                         ♠ A K J 10
    ♡ 10 7 6 5 3                    ♡ K Q 9 4
    ◇ 10 8 5                        ◇ J 4
    ♣ 9 4                           ♣ 7 5 3
                    ♠ 9 3
                    ♡ A J
                    ◇ K 9 7 2
                    ♣ A J 10 8 6
```

Before partner can begin his remonstrances about the bidding East
is telling the old tale—he pulled the wrong card, he thought the spade
had been led, the light was bad . . . .

Post-mortem

The type of pseudo-squeeze used on this hand is one of the least-
known arts in the game. For it to have a chance of success, declarer
needs to have two one-card threats against the right-hand opponent.
There must be a side suit in which dummy and declarer have the same
length. At trick 12 a card of this suit must be led from dummy which,
from the point of view of an unobservant defender, may or may not be a
winner.

31. A Superfluous Nugget

It isn't my birthday but I pick up one of the best hands I have ever held:

♠ A K Q J 5 4 ♡ A K Q ◇ A Q 9 4 ♣ —

It is rubber bridge, too, and I am playing with a good partner. I am fourth to speak, with no one vulnerable. Not surprisingly, there are three passes, and I open **two clubs**, the conventional bid of the Acol system which my partner and I are playing. He responds **two diamonds** and, putting one of the system's rarer conventions to use, I bid **three spades**. That is a demand for Aces. Its advantage here is that on the next round I can ask for specific Kings.

Partner responds **3NT**, denying an Ace. I then bid **four diamonds**, according to plan. If he has the King of diamonds he will bid five diamonds, while if he has a singleton diamond and some spade support he may jump to five spades, for my earlier bid of three spades set the suit.

None of these good things is forthcoming. He gives me just **four spades** but I am not going to give in. I shall bid **five spades.** Partner knows that the only side suit in which I am interested is diamonds and he will give me six if he has anything in his hand to suggest that I won't lose two diamond tricks. At last he comes to life with **six spades**.

Our auction has been:

South	West	North	East
—	pass	pass	pass
2♣	pass	2◇	pass
3♠	pass	3NT	pass
4◇	pass	4♠	pass
5♠	pass	6♠	pass
pass	pass		

West leads the 3 of spades and I contemplate the following dummy:

♠ 10 8 7
♡ J 10 7 6 3
◇ 6 2
♣ Q J 3

♠ 3 led

♠ A K Q J 5 4
♡ A K Q
◇ A Q 9 4
♣ —

We had to explain the various conventional bids to our opponents as we went along and while, in a technical way, I am quite proud of our auction it seems to have given them a clue to the best lead. On any other lead I could have ruffed a couple of diamonds. However, let us see what happens to the 7 of spades. East plays the 2 and I follow with the 4.

Now if I finesse a diamond and it loses they will play another trump. That won't matter if the trumps are 2 – 2, but if the trumps are 3 – 1 I won't be able to make the slam by ruffing diamonds. Can I do anything with the hearts? I could draw a second trump and play A K Q of hearts. If no one ruffed I would have enough tricks.

"What does it matter if the third round is ruffed?" did I hear you say? I thought that for a moment, but count the tricks again. Suppose that the trumps are 3 – 1 and that the third round of hearts is ruffed. Then when I enter dummy with the third spade there will be only two hearts left and I'll still have to take the diamond finesse.

I keep on getting so near, there must be some answer to this hand. If it weren't for that block in hearts there wouldn't be any difficulty. If I could bury that Queen of hearts, for example. Is that an idea? I believe it is! If I play a club and discard the Queen of hearts I shall make six spades, five hearts (so long as the second round is not ruffed) and a diamond.

I play the 3 of clubs from dummy, East plays the Ace and I match it with the Ace of hearts. (The Ace looks sportier than the Queen!) East leads a diamond and I go up with the Ace. Now I lead a second round of spades, for if the spades are 2 – 2 I can bear the hearts to be 4 – 1. As expected, East shows out on the second spade. I cash K Q of hearts, everybody following. Then I play to dummy's 10 of spades and my three diamonds go away on the J 10 7 of hearts.

These manœuvres were necessary, for this was the full hand:

```
                    ♠ 10 8 7
                    ♡ J 10 7 6 3
                    ◇ 6 2
                    ♣ Q J 3
♠ 9 6 3                              ♠ 2
♡ 8 2                                ♡ 9 5 4
◇ K J 8 5                            ◇ 10 7 3
♣ K 10 6 5                           ♣ A 9 8 7 4 2
                    ♠ A K Q J 5 4
                    ♡ A K Q
                    ◇ A Q 9 4
                    ♣ —
```

Post-mortem

The bidding convention that we used on this hand is valuable on occasions and can be adapted to any two club system. The jump rebid, following a two club opening, sets the suit and asks partner to name his Aces immediately. Any subsequent enquiry asks for Kings. It may be possible, as on this hand, to direct attention to third-round control as well.

As to the play, the combination of winner-on-loser and unblock is rare but elegant.

32. Submarine Journey

Playing in a multiple team contest against opponents who are strangers to me, I hold:

♠ A Q 9 5 ♡ A 4 3 ◇ K 7 6 ♣ A 9 2

We are vulnerable, they not. East, on my right, deals and opens **three diamonds**. This is a familiar situation in which one cannot be sure of doing the right thing. However, it would be timid to pass, so I **double**. My partner and I play a double at this level to show a good all-round hand. West comes in with **three hearts** and this appears to give partner a problem. Eventually he bids **four diamonds**, the enemy suit, and East passes. With my defensive hand I don't like the way things are going, but all I can do is bid **four spades**. This is passed all round, so the bidding has been:

South	West	North	East
—	—	—	3◇
double	3♡	4◇	pass
4♣	pass	pass	pass

West leads the 5 of diamonds and partner's hand, like mine, turns out to be balanced:

```
                    ♠ K 6 4
                    ♡ 9 5 2
                    ◇ A 8 3
                    ♣ K Q 7 6

◇ 5 led

                    ♠ A Q 9 5
                    ♡ A 4 3
                    ◇ K 7 6
                    ♣ A 9 2
```

Yes, we would have done better to defend and pick up a safe 500 or more that way. Four spades will be all right if the suits break evenly, but probably they won't. To begin with, I can't see anything better than to take the first trick with the King of diamonds and test the trumps.

All follow to the first two rounds of spades but on the third round East discards a diamond. So West has four spades and, I assume from the bidding, six hearts. That means the clubs will probably be 4 – 2. I am one trick short, but if East has the long diamonds and long clubs perhaps I can squeeze him. To do that I must rectify the count, as they say, by losing three tricks before the squeeze begins. That can be done easily enough by giving up the trump and ducking two rounds of hearts.

To avoid complications I play the fourth trump right away, discarding a diamond from the table. West exits with a club and I win with the Queen in dummy. Now, according to plan, I lead a low heart. East puts in the Queen and I duck. West considers whether to overtake but eventually plays low. The position is now:

♠ —
♡ 9 5
◇ A
♣ K 7 6

♠ —
♡ A 4
◇ 7 6
♣ A 9

East exits with a diamond to dummy's Ace, West discarding a heart. (Had East played a club at this point I would have had to play the diamond myself before ducking the heart.) I lead a low heart from dummy and duck again. West exits with a club to my Ace and now the Ace of hearts squeezes East in the minor suits. I have made the contract for the loss of two hearts and one spade, the full hand being:

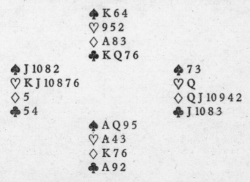

```
            ♠ K 6 4
            ♡ 9 5 2
            ◇ A 8 3
            ♣ K Q 7 6
♠ J 10 8 2                ♠ 7 3
♡ K J 10 8 7 6            ♡ Q
◇ 5                       ◇ Q J 10 9 4 2
♣ 5 4                     ♣ J 10 8 3
            ♠ A Q 9 5
            ♡ A 4 3
            ◇ K 7 6
            ♣ A 9 2
```

Post-mortem

The hand contains a trap that is not mentioned in the narrative. When declarer sees the possibility of developing a submarine squeeze by ducking two rounds of hearts, he may think of exiting with a heart instead of with the last trump. That will not matter if West leads the Jack of spades, as a player with the master trump will usually do. But if West is shrewd enough to continue hearts instead the timing will be different. East will have room for an extra discard and South will not be able to bring any pressure to bear.

33. No Second Chance

Playing rubber bridge against experienced opponents, I hold:

♠ Q 10 9 7 6 2 ♡ A 8 3 ◇ J 3 ♣ K 4

With both sides vulnerable, my partner deals and bids **one club**. East passes and I respond **one spade**. West comes in with **two diamonds** and partner raises to **two spades**. There should be a fair play for game, so I go straight to **four spades** and all pass. The bidding has been:

South	West	North	East
—	—	1♣	pass
1♠	2◇	2♠	pass
4♠	pass	pass	pass

West opens the King of diamonds and partner puts down:

♠ A K J
♡ J 7 5 2
◇ Q 5
♣ A 8 6 3

◇ K led

♠ Q 10 9 7 6 2
♡ A 8 3
◇ J 3
♣ K 4

Not an ideal dummy, as we seem to be in danger of losing two diamonds and two hearts. West cashes a second diamond and East, having played the 9 on the first round, completes an echo with the 6. West switches to the Jack of clubs and I let this run up to the King.

Now how am I going to avoid losing two tricks in hearts? West may have K Q alone. Failing that, there are elimination possibilities if either defender has a doubleton K x or Q x. As West has the long diamonds he is more likely to be short in hearts. Then of course he may be able to unblock—not if he has K 10 or Q 10, but with K x or Q x he can throw his honour under the Ace.

I have to consider what is the best point at which to lay down the Ace of hearts. Obviously I don't want to wait until the possibility of an elimination is obvious. At the same time West might regard it as suspicious if I were to lay down the Ace of hearts immediately. I think a rather more plausible sequence would be to cross to the King of spades and then come back to the Ace of hearts as though I were regaining the lead for a possible trump finesse.

All follow when I play a spade to the King and when a heart is returned to the Ace East plays the 4 and West the 9. Now I have to assume that West has failed to unblock from Q 9 or K 9. There are two ways of proceeding with the elimination play. If West has a singleton spade and three clubs, together with seven diamonds and two hearts, the best line is to play a club to the Ace and ruff a club and then to exit with a heart. On the other hand, if West has two trumps and two clubs he may well think of discarding his heart honour when I ruff the third club. But if he has a singleton trump and three clubs he may fail to discard the heart when I play a second trump. So I'm going to play another round of trumps at this point.

West follows to the second trump and so does East. These cards are left:

$$\spadesuit \text{ J}$$
$$\heartsuit \text{ J 7 5}$$
$$\diamondsuit \text{ —}$$
$$\clubsuit \text{ A 8 6}$$

$$\spadesuit \text{ Q 10 9 7}$$
$$\heartsuit \text{ 8 3}$$
$$\diamondsuit \text{ —}$$
$$\clubsuit \text{ 4}$$

I play the Ace of clubs and all follow. A third club would be a mistake now because I am taking West to be 2 – 2 – 7 – 2 with a top heart left, and I mustn't give him the chance to discard that heart. After the Ace of clubs I lead a low heart. West wins with the Queen and leads a diamond. That gives me a ruff and discard, so I make the contract for the loss of two diamonds and one heart. West could not recover from his first mistake of not dropping the Queen of hearts under the Ace, for this was the full hand:

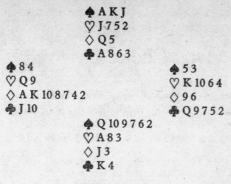

♠ A K J
♥ J 7 5 2
♦ Q 5
♣ A 8 6 3

♠ 8 4
♥ Q 9
♦ A K 10 8 7 4 2
♣ J 10

♠ 5 3
♥ K 10 6 4
♦ 9 6
♣ Q 9 7 5 2

♠ Q 10 9 7 6 2
♥ A 8 3
♦ J 3
♣ K 4

Post-mortem

The first point about this hand was the way in which the play of the Ace of hearts was timed. The elimination possibilities contained in the heart situation are well known and so is the defensive play of unblocking with an honour. Therefore declarer has to consider a sequence of play that may cause the defenders to take their eye off the ball.

The other point is that declarer's count of the hand showed that a third round of clubs before the throw-in would be a mistake. Had a third club been played West would not have failed to disembarrass himself of the Queen of hearts.

34. Choice Deferred

My partner in this game of rubber bridge is a somewhat unreliable bidder and the opposition is not particularly strong. In third position I hold:

♠ 8 6 5 3 2   ♡ 9   ◇ A Q 5 3   ♣ A J 6

It is game all and my partner opens **one heart**. With the opponents silent, I respond **one spade** and partner raises to **three spades.**

This is a situation I never care for. My two Aces suggest a slam but the trump holding is unsatisfactory. I feel that I must make one try, so I bid **four clubs** to see what that produces.

It produces a prompt 4NT, Blackwood. I suppose I must see it through. After **five hearts** partner gives me no more leeway. He goes straight to **six spades.**

The bidding has been:

South	West	North	East
—	—	1♡	pass
1♠	pass	3♠	pass
4♣	pass	4NT	pass
5♡	pass	6♠	pass
pass	pass		

West leads the 9 of diamonds and partner's hand is not exactly what I wanted to see:

```
                    ♠ A K J
                    ♡ A Q 7 4 2
                    ◇ K 6
                    ♣ Q 7 4

        ◇ 9 led

                    ♠ 8 6 5 3 2
                    ♡ 9
                    ◇ A Q 5 3
                    ♣ A J 6
```

If I play a straightforward game shall I have enough tricks? That is, suppose I win with King of diamonds, cash two spades and ruff the fourth diamond. I'll have to lose a trump and then I'll need the heart finesse or three club tricks. An end-play may develop but it is rather nebulous. Instead, how about ruffing some hearts with my small trumps? If I do get overruffed it may be by the hand that has the long trumps. If by any chance I can bring down the King of hearts in three rounds I shall have enough tricks without the club finesse, assuming that the spades are 3 – 2.

I win the diamond lead in hand, cross to Ace of hearts, ruff a heart and return to the Ace of spades. On this trick East drops the 9. When a third heart is played from the table East ruffs with the Queen of spades. That alters the complexion of the hand. Let's look at the position after East's ruff:

♠ K J
♡ Q 7
◇ K
♣ Q 7 4

♠ 8 6 5
♡ —
◇ Q 5 3
♣ A J 6

I still have to discard and I am not sure what to play. East had a doubleton heart and, I imagine, a doubleton spade, for he dropped the 9 on the first round and is now ruffing with the Queen. He could be false-carding but he is not a particularly subtle player and I don't think it's likely.

If my count of the spades and hearts is correct then East must have length in both minor suits. That means there is no chance of bringing down a doubleton King of clubs. Furthermore, if West has the last two trumps I cannot ruff a diamond without establishing his 10 of spades. Whether I discard a diamond or a club I am going to be a trick short, even assuming that the club finesse is right.

It seems an odd thing to do with three trumps in my hand and two in dummy, but could there be any advantage in underruffing? As I am playing some sort of reverse dummy and can ruff another heart, the trick should come back. If I preserve my holding in diamonds and clubs, I may well be able to squeeze East.

Yes, that's the play. In the diagram position I underruff with the 5 of spades. East exits with the Jack of diamonds and I win in dummy with the King. I play a heart from table and East discards a diamond.

I ruff and return to the King of spades, and now East discards a club. This is the position when the last trump is played:

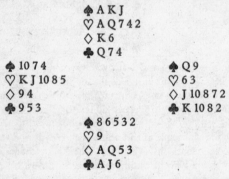

```
            ♠ J
            ♡ Q
            ◇ —
            ♣ Q 7 4


            ♠ —
            ♡ —
            ◇ Q 5
            ♣ A J 6
```

On the lead of the Jack of spades East is plainly in trouble. When eventually he discards a club I throw my diamond. A club finesse follows and when the King falls under the Ace on the next trick I make the remainder, having lost only to the Queen of trumps. This was the full hand:

```
                    ♠ A K J
                    ♡ A Q 7 4 2
                    ◇ K 6
                    ♣ Q 7 4
    ♠ 10 7 4                       ♠ Q 9
    ♡ K J 10 8 5                   ♡ 6 3
    ◇ 9 4                          ◇ J 10 8 7 2
    ♣ 9 5 3                        ♣ K 10 8 2
                    ♠ 8 6 5 3 2
                    ♡ 9
                    ◇ A Q 5 3
                    ♣ A J 6
```

Post-mortem

The underruff to preserve possibilities of a squeeze is uncommon but worth noting. As the cards lie, of course, the contract can be made more simply in a number of ways. In fact, if declarer finesses the Queen of hearts and plays off A K of spades he can squeeze East for thirteen tricks.

As the play went, a clever defender in East's position would have declined the opportunity to ruff the third heart. In due course declarer would finesse the Jack of spades and then the timing for a squeeze would be wrong.

35. Bold Conclusion

On this hand from a mixed pairs event my partner and the opponents are all good players. I hold as dealer:

♠ A 10 6   ♡ A J 3   ◇ K Q 9 7 4   ♣ A J

We are vulnerable but the hand is too strong for 1NT according to my methods, so I open **one diamond**. The opponents are silent and partner, after some deliberation, responds **two diamonds**. Now I jump to **3NT**. The bidding has been brief:

North	West	South	East
—	—	1◇	pass
2◇	pass	3NT	pass
pass	pass		

West opens the 6 of hearts. Observing that with anyone else she would have responded one spade, partner puts down:

```
              ♠ Q 7 4 2
              ♡ Q
              ◇ J 8 3 2
              ♣ Q 10 5 4

♡ 6 led

              ♠ A 10 6
              ♡ A J 3
              ◇ K Q 9 7 4
              ♣ A J
```

Partner is right in her estimate that I much prefer a response of two diamonds to one spade. I can see no sense whatsoever in bidding bad suits on bad hands when there is a sound alternative.

Dummy's Queen of hearts holds the first trick, East playing the 2. Now I can count four probable tricks in diamonds, two in hearts and two black Aces. Obviously the safe way to play for a ninth trick is to take a club finesse before clearing the Ace of diamonds. If the finesse loses, West will not be able to continue hearts to advantage.

At trick 2 therefore I finesse the Jack of clubs and it holds the trick.

That doesn't tell me who has the King because West would probably hold off in any event. Now I lead the King of diamonds, West plays the 10 and East the 5. On the next round of diamonds West discards a low club and East tops dummy's Jack with the Ace. East returns the 9 of hearts.

I am safe for nine tricks now and the question is whether to go up with the Ace of hearts, keeping the Jack as an exit card, or to hold up the Ace until the third round. It seems clear from the play that West began with six hearts to the K 10 and East with three small. The prospects for an end-play are somewhat uncertain. I think it would be better to hold up so as to exhaust East of hearts and then see how they discard on the diamonds. West tops the Jack of hearts with the King and returns a heart, East following suit. After two more rounds of diamonds the position is as follows:

♠ Q 7 4
♡ —
♢ —
♣ Q 10

♠ A 10 6
♡ —
♢ 7
♣ A

On the last two tricks West has discarded a heart and the 5 of spades and East has thrown a club. On the fifth diamond West discards the 8 of spades, North the 4 and East the 3.

The problem now is whether I can afford to play for an overtrick by taking two rounds of spades and not cashing the Ace of clubs. First I'll see what happens on the Ace of spades. West follows with the Jack and East with the 9. Now if I play a spade and West has the King of spades plus two hearts I shall be one down. On the other hand, if East has the King of spades I can make an overtrick.

Apart from the fact that West might have overcalled if he had held four spades and six hearts, there are two strong indications from the play. West's first discard was a club. Surely, if he had been 4-6-1-2, he would have let go a spade first. Secondly, there are still three clubs out and it is most unlikely that East has them all. His natural play would be to discard down to K x of clubs, not K x x.

At total-point scoring I might not risk it, but in a pairs one has to follow one's judgment on such occasions. I play a spade and all is well. East has the King and I make the last two tricks with the Ace of clubs and 10 of spades, scoring an overtrick. This was the full hand:

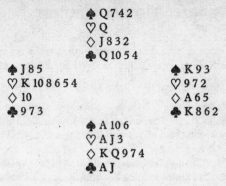

♠ Q 7 4 2
♡ Q
◇ J 8 3 2
♣ Q 10 5 4

♠ J 8 5
♡ K 10 8 6 5 4
◇ 10
♣ 9 7 3

♠ K 9 3
♡ 9 7 2
◇ A 6 5
♣ K 8 6 2

♠ A 10 6
♡ A J 3
◇ K Q 9 7 4
♣ A J

Post-mortem

Taking the club finesse at trick 2 was a matter of ordinary technique. If declarer plays first on diamonds and the hearts are cleared by a lead through the A J, there is no sure way to develop a ninth trick.

The ending is typical of many where the play for an overtrick, though superficially risky, is safe enough if the right inferences are drawn. Most players in these situations are either too lazy to work out the lie of the cards or too cowardly to put their conclusions to the test. The right approach is to take the risk that once in twenty times one has misread the position. The overtrick on the other nineteen will fully compensate in match-pointed events.

West's discarding on this hand was not in fact the best. If he throws all his clubs and keeps one more spade the lie of the cards cannot be read with any certainty.

36. Almost Caught

This hand is from a pairs contest where all the players are supposedly of master class. Towards the end of the session I hold as dealer:

♠ 8 ♡ A Q 10 ◇ A 10 9 7 6 3 ♣ A Q 4

We are vulnerable and I open **one diamond.** West passes and my partner raises to **three diamonds.** That's a natural bid with us, not forcing. I could bid three hearts, which might lead to 3NT, but I am really too good to stop there. Playing match-points I naturally don't intend to languish in five diamonds, so I'll go straight to **six diamonds,** giving nothing away. Our bidding has been short if not accurate:

South	West	North	East
1◇	pass	3◇	pass
6◇	pass	pass	pass

West leads the 10 of spades and partner's hand is nothing to cheer about:

> ♠ A J 4
> ♡ 7 6 4 2
> ◇ Q 5 4 2
> ♣ K 10

♠ 10 led

> ♠ 8
> ♡ A Q 10
> ◇ A 10 9 7 6 3
> ♣ A Q 4

He had rather an awkward bid over one diamond. He is too good for two diamonds or 1NT and to respond one heart on 7 x x x is not part of our methods. I'm sure some of them will be playing this hand in four hearts, at that. I've seen it many times.

To make six diamonds I need a finesse or two. There is a safety play to lose only one trick in the trump suit but this is no moment for such luxuries. As there may be some sort of elimination ending I plan to take the spade Ace, ruff a spade with the 6 and then lay down the trump Ace.

Alas, East shows out on the Ace of diamonds, discarding a spade. I follow with the 7 of diamonds. West goes up with the King and plays a third spade, which I ruff with the 9.

With very little risk now I can play for an elimination ending that will save me from going down two even if both heart honours are wrong. I play three rounds of clubs, discarding a heart from the table as the opponents follow suit. Then I lead the 10 of diamonds to dummy's Queen, reaching this position:

```
          ♠ —
          ♡ 7 6 4
          ◇ 5
          ♣ —


          ♠ —
          ♡ A Q 10
          ◇ 3
          ♣ —
```

Now I lead a heart from dummy and finesse the 10, expecting to lose the trick and concede one down, but the 10 wins! Am I going to make this contract after all? I cross to the 5 of diamonds, West discarding a heart and East a club. When I play a heart from dummy at trick 12, East puts on the 8—and I nearly break my wrist pulling back the Queen which I had ready to play.

What's this 8 of hearts? I thought I was finessing East for the K J but I can see what has happened. Expecting me to finesse the heart again, West has come down to the singleton King of hearts and the thirteenth spade. It was a clever plan to put me two down and would surely have succeeded had East played his part by putting in the Jack. Feeling quite sorry for West, I go up with the Ace of hearts and drop the King, making an "impossible" contract. This was the full hand:

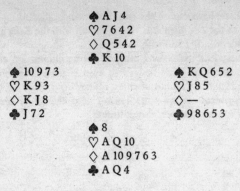

♠ A J 4
♥ 7 6 4 2
♦ Q 5 4 2
♣ K 10

♠ 10 9 7 3
♥ K 9 3
♦ K J 8
♣ J 7 2

♠ K Q 6 5 2
♥ J 8 5
♦ —
♣ 9 8 6 5 3

♠ 8
♥ A Q 10
♦ A 10 9 7 6 3
♣ A Q 4

Post-mortem

That was bad luck for West. Towards the end of a pairs when one
has not been doing too well is the time to experiment with a desperate
play of that sort. Had East been awake and played the Jack of hearts at
trick 12, South would have finessed the Queen and West would have
made the last two tricks to score 200 and a "top" on the board.

Note, meanwhile, South's careful preservation of the trump 3 as an
entry to dummy.

37. Show of Disinterest

In a team-of-four match against opponents of average strength I hold as dealer:

♠ A K Q 9 2   ♡ A 10   ◇ A K 3   ♣ J 10 4

We are vulnerable, the opponents not. As the spades are reasonably self-supporting I fancy opening **2NT**. Partner raises to **3NT** and all pass, making a simple auction:

South	West	North	East
2NT	pass	3NT	pass
pass	pass		

West opens the 6 of hearts and I see that partner had little to spare for his raise:

                    ♠ 7 5 4
                    ♡ Q J 9
                    ◇ J 9 8 7 2
                    ♣ 9 5
    ♡ 6 led

                    ♠ A K Q 9 2
                    ♡ A 10
                    ◇ A K 3
                    ♣ J 10 4

I go up with the Queen of hearts from dummy and East plays the 5. As I shall be home if the spades break, I play a spade to the Ace, East dropping the 10. On the King of spades East discards the 2 of hearts. I am not quite sure about the heart position yet, but I may as well see what happens on the Queen of spades. This time East throws the 3 of clubs.

Now there are two possibilities. I can play off Ace and King of diamonds in the hope of dropping the Queen, or I can give up the fourth spade and hope they won't find their club tricks. In view of the discarding—East's signal in hearts and his discard of a low club—it seems most unlikely that West, who did not lead a club originally, will switch to that suit now. Establishing another spade will give me only eight tricks, but meanwhile I'll be forcing East to two more discards and something favourable may arise.

West wins the fourth round of spades with the Jack and I discard a diamond from the table. Though an old trick, this show of disinterest in dummy's anaemic diamond suit may persuade an opponent with Q x x to unguard the suit. For the moment, however, East throws the 6 of clubs. West, as expected, continued with the 4 of hearts, East plays the 7 and I win with the Ace. These are the remaining cards:

♠ —
♡ J
◇ J 9 8 7
♣ 9 5

♠ 2
♡ —
◇ A K 3
♣ J 10 4

On the fifth West spade discards the 7 of clubs. To throw another diamond from dummy would be overdoing it, I think. A declarer with something like A x would normally keep four to the Jack in the opposite hand. So I discard a club and East, after some thought, lets go the 8 of clubs.

Now again I have to consider whether or not to play off the top diamonds. Despite my puny attempt at deception by throwing a diamond from table, neither defender has thrown one and I find that a little sinister. East was not too happy about relinquishing this last club, and if he had had three diamonds not headed by the Queen he would have thrown one of those in preference. There are only four clubs still out and I am inclined to place East with a singleton honour, together with two winning hearts and, very likely, three diamonds to the Queen. If East has the Ace of clubs, and the rest of my assessment is correct, I can end-play him for sure. And if East has the King or Queen, it's still possible that West will fail to go up with the Ace in second position. At any rate I feel so certain the Queen of diamonds is guarded that I plan to exit with a club.

As I don't want to encourage West to play an honour, I lead a low club toward dummy's 9. West plays the 2 and East wins with the King. East cashes the King and 8 of hearts, and I discard the J 10 of clubs.

That makes four tricks for the defence. East exits with the 5 of diamonds at trick 11. I hold my breath and let it ride to dummy's Jack—successfully, for the full hand is:

♠ 7 5 4
♡ Q J 9
◇ J 9 8 7 2
♣ 9 5

♠ J 8 6 3
♡ 6 4 3
◇ 6 4
♣ A Q 7 2

♠ 10
♡ K 8 7 5 2
◇ Q 10 5
♣ K 8 6 3

♠ A K Q 9 2
♡ A 10
◇ A K 3
♣ J 10 4

Post-mortem

The defence made some mistakes here, but to some extent they were induced by declarer's bidding and play. The points to note are:

1. East's discards on the second and third rounds of spades made it safe for declarer to force out the fourth spade even though the clubs were wide open.

2. As the play proceeded, it became increasingly likely that East was guarding the diamond Queen. The sequence of his discards suggested, moreover, that he had five hearts and four clubs.

3. West could have defeated the contract, of course, by going up with his Ace of clubs from A Q x on the club lead. That was a difficult play and the main fault was East's in coming down to the King of clubs single instead of a low one. Another reason why East should have kept a low club and not the King is that partner's clubs might have been headed by the A J.

38. Rash Venture

In a keenly fought game of rubber bridge my side is not vulnerable and has nothing below the line. The opponents are vulnerable and have a part score of 40. I hold as dealer:

♠ A Q 2   ♡ 8 5 2   ◇ K 4   ♣ A 10 8 7 3

In these part score situations I like to open 1NT when possible, but my partner has insisted on a strong notrump throughout, so perhaps that would be unwise. Instead, I shall venture a psychic **one heart**. If ever there is a time to make such a bid, this is it—not vulnerable against vulnerable opponents who have a part score.

West overcalls with **one spade** and my partner bids **two spades**. I don't altogether like the sound of that. No doubt he is going to raise the hearts in a moment! After a pass by East I bid **2NT**. West competes again with **three clubs** and now my partner bids **three diamonds**. East appears to quiver for a moment before passing.

I'm slightly tempted to pass three diamonds before he puts me into six hearts or something of that sort. However, it's possible that if he hears me bid notrumps again he will realize that my hearts are more or less non-existent. So I bid **3NT** and West passes. Partner considers for a while, then bids **four hearts**. As expected, East **doubles**. All pass and this is the sad story of the auction:

South	West	North	East
1♡	1♠	2♠	pass
2NT	3♣	3◇	pass
3NT	pass	4♡	double
pass	pass	pass	

120

West leads the 7 of hearts and partner puts down:

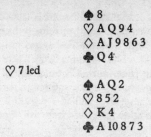

♠ 8
♡ A Q 9 4
◇ A J 9 8 6 3
♣ Q 4

♡ 7 led

♠ A Q 2
♡ 8 5 2
◇ K 4
♣ A 10 8 7 3

One thing about this bidding is that it isn't difficult to place the cards. West must have at least six spades (because they have not been supported) and probably five clubs. He may have two red singletons or, slightly more probable on the lead, a doubleton heart and a void in diamonds.

I play a low heart from dummy and East wins with the Jack, no doubt a false card. East returns the 5 of spades. I'm not going to be able to draw trumps and establish diamonds, so I may as well make as many tricks as I can by ruffing. I go up with the Ace of spades and ruff the 2 of spades with dummy's 9 of hearts.

If West's distribution is 6 – 1 – 1 – 5 my best line now will be to take two diamond ruffs in my hand. But I think it's more likely that he is 6 – 2 – 0 – 5. With two singletons he might well have led the diamond and also, if East had had five trumps, it would have been better defence on his part to return a trump at trick 2. To confirm that view, I cash the Ace of hearts. East plays the 3 and West follows with the 6. Now I play a club to the Ace and ruff the Queen of spades with dummy's last heart, West playing the King of spades and East the Jack. That leaves the cards as follows:

♠ —
♡ —
◇ A J 9 8 6 3
♣ Q

♠ —
♡ 8
◇ K 4
♣ 10 8 7 3

This hand is not going to be a calamity, after all. I can play it almost

as double dummy from now on. East must have K 10 of hearts and all
five diamonds.

In the diagram position I lead the 8 of diamonds from dummy. If
East plays low I'm going to let that run, then come to hand with the
King of diamonds and exit with a trump. East seems to be aware of
that, for he puts in the 10, which I take with the King. There are several
ways of making three more tricks now. Choosing one of the more
artistic, I lead the 4 of diamonds to the Ace and return the Jack. East
covers with the Queen and instead of ruffing I discard a club. East
makes his two good hearts and then has to lead from the 7 5 of diamonds
into dummy's 9 6.

That leaves me one down—not such a bad result when one looks at
the full diagram:

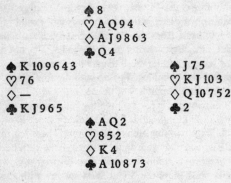

Post-mortem

Once declarer had taken note of the likely distribution, the hand
played surprisingly well. East thought he might have saved a trick by
unblocking with the 10 of hearts under the Ace and keeping the 3 as an
exit card. (South had played the 2 on the first trick.) That would not
have affected the result so long as South took care not to be left in his
own hand with nothing but clubs to lead. By declining to ruff the
Queen of diamonds South forced East to retain the lead. East was end-
played and eventually had to return two diamond tricks for one.

39. Fortune Accepted

My partner in this pairs tournament is an earnest performer and the opponents, so far as I know, not especially formidable. With neither side vulnerable, I pick up as dealer:

♠ A Q 9 4 3   ♡ A K 3   ◇ K 10 6   ♣ A 4

As we are doing fairly well at this stage of the contest I reject any notion of 2NT and open an orthodox **one spade**. West overcalls with **two diamonds** and this is passed by North and East. I could double now or bid 2NT. The **double** is slightly better as partner could have a weak hand with long hearts. Over my double West competes again with **three diamonds**. Partner thinks awhile, consults the ceiling, and eventually gives me **three spades**. I have an idea that my hand isn't quite as good as it looks, but I must go on to **four spades**.

The bidding has been:

South	West	North	East
1♠	2◇	pass	pass
double	3◇	3♠	pass
4♠	pass	pass	pass

West opens the 5 of hearts and a little nervously partner puts down:

♠ K 10 6 5
♡ J 7 4
◇ 5 4
♣ 10 8 7 5

♡ 5 led

♠ A Q 9 4 3
♡ A K 3
◇ K 10 6
♣ A 4

The lead could be anything, but as East is not likely to have a doubleton Queen of hearts I may as well put up dummy's Jack. A little to my surprise, it holds the trick. I play a spade to the Ace and all follow.

The contract is in no danger now, for I can draw trumps and lose, at most, two diamonds and a club. There is a chance for an overtrick if I can end-play West in clubs and force him to lead diamonds. He is undoubtedly short in clubs and if he has K Q alone, for example, or the singleton King, I may be able to manage it.

Against very strong opponents I would have to be careful about the sequence of play lest West have an opportunity to discard a high club. I don't think that the present West is likely to perform any prodigies of unblocking, so I will take the simple course and draw a second trump with the Queen.

The trumps turn out to be 2 – 2. I play off two top hearts and again all follow, West playing the Queen on the third round. The following cards are left:

    ♠ K 10
    ♡ —
    ◊ 5 4
    ♣ 10 8 7 5

    ♠ 9 4 3
    ♡ —
    ◊ K 10 8
    ♣ A 4

Could West be 2 – 3 – 6 – 2? Just possible, if his clubs were K Q. But then he might have led a club in preference to a heart from Q x x. It is altogether more likely that he has seven diamonds and a singleton club. After all, he did bid three diamonds very much under the gun.

If he has a singleton King of clubs I can just play a small club from hand. But he may have a singleton Queen, and in that case it is better to lead the club from dummy before East realizes what is happening. It is true that by crossing to dummy I give West a chance to disembarrass himself of the high club, but I don't expect him to do that.

In the diagram position I lead a spade to the King, West discarding a diamond. On the lead of the 7 of clubs East plays the 9 and I duck, as planned. West wins with the Queen and has to play diamonds, so I end up with an overtrick, the full hand being:

```
              ♠ K 10 6 5
              ♡ J 7 4
              ◇ 5 4
              ♣ 10 8 7 5
♠ 8 2                        ♠ J 7
♡ Q 9 5                      ♡ 10 8 6 2
◇ A Q J 9 7 3 2              ◇ 8
♣ Q                          ♣ K J 9 6 3 2
              ♠ A Q 9 4 3
              ♡ A K 3
              ◇ K 10 6
              ♣ A 4
```

Post-mortem

Three factors contributed to the overtrick—a lucky lead, a count of West's distribution, and the strategic move of leading the club from dummy rather than from hand.

Both defenders could have done better—West by throwing the Queen of clubs on the third trump, and East by going up with the King when the club was led. Neither play was at all easy.

40. Retaining the Loser

My partner on this occasion is a stranger of whose methods I know nothing. It is the first hand of the rubber and I hold:

♠ K Q 9 8 7 3   ♡ K 7 2   ◇ Q 9 8 5   ♣ —

Partner opens **one club** and after a pass by East I respond **one spade**. West passes and partner introduces **two hearts**. Whether that is meant to show a big hand or not I don't know, but I can't bid less than **three spades**. West suddenly interposes a **double**. Partner considers awhile and finally passes. I have nothing more to say, so the bidding has been:

South	West	North	East
—	—	1♣	pass
1♠	pass	2♡	pass
3♠	double	pass	pass
pass			

West leads the Ace of clubs and without any sign of remorse partner puts down:

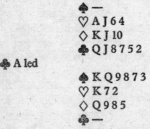

```
            ♠ —
            ♡ A J 6 4
            ◇ K J 10
            ♣ Q J 8 7 5 2
♣ A led
            ♠ K Q 9 8 7 3
            ♡ K 7 2
            ◇ Q 9 8 5
            ♣ —
```

If that's how he bids I'm glad he's not at the wheel in four hearts doubled. Not that three spades is likely to be a success. I must make what tricks I can in the side suits, together with a few trumps. After ruffing the first club I play a diamond to the King. This holds and I ruff another club. (Although West normally leads the King from A K, I imagine he is false-carding on this occasion. I don't think he would lead the unsupported Ace of dummy's suit.)

Faintly hoping that West will let it pass, I lead a small diamond to the J 10 but West has seen his partner's 2 on the preceding round and goes up with the Ace. He switches to the 8 of hearts. It's unlikely to win but I put in dummy's Jack. East covers with the Queen and I win with the King. Both opponents follow when I play a diamond to the Jack. When I ruff a third round of clubs West drops the King.

It's going as well as can be expected so far. Now I play to the Ace of hearts in dummy and the position is as follows:

♠ —
♡ 6 4
♢ —
♣ Q J 8

♠ K Q 9
♡ 7
♢ Q
♣ —

West is know to have begun with three diamonds and three clubs. He could have four spades and a heart left, but more likely he has nothing but trumps. The way the bidding was going, he wouldn't have doubled three spades without a commanding hand.

The more trumps he has, the better my chance. I have lost only one trick so far and now I must decide what to throw on the Queen of clubs. The losing heart is the obvious card. Or is it? West will ruff the club and probably exit with a middle trump—or possibly with a low trump to his partner's 10. But if I retain the heart I can force West to ruff it at the next trick with no fear that East will be able to overruff and then play through me.

On the Queen of clubs, therefore, I discard the master diamond. West ruffs low and exits with the Jack of spades. I win with the King and play the heart. West has to ruff and concede a ninth trick to the Queen of spades, the full hand being:

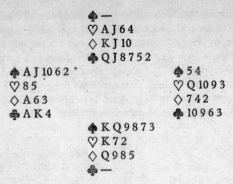

```
              ♣ —
              ♡ A J 6 4
              ◇ K J 10
              ♣ Q J 8 7 5 2
♠ A J 10 6 2 ·            ♠ 5 4
♡ 8 5                     ♡ Q 10 9 3
◇ A 6 3                   ◇ 7 4 2
♣ A K 4                   ♣ 10 9 6 3
              ♠ K Q 9 8 7 3
              ♡ K 7 2
              ◇ Q 9 8 5
              ♣ —
```

I was able to congratulate my partner on his discretion in passing three spades doubled.

"Oh, I wasn't going to bid 3NT with a void of your suit," he answered virtuously.

Post-mortem

Had South played inaccurately at the finish, an interesting defensive point would have arisen. This was the position round the table five cards from the end:

```
              ♠ —
              ♡ 6 4
              ◇ —
              ♣ Q J 8
♠ A J 10 6 2             ♠ 5 4
♡ —                      ♡ 10 9
◇ —                      ◇ —
♣ —                      ♣ 10
              ♠ K Q 9
              ♡ 7
              ◇ Q
              ♣ —
```

If declarer discards a heart on the Queen of clubs, West must ruff with the 6, not the 2. He exits with the Jack of spades to South's King. When South leads the diamond West is able to ruff low and East overruffs with the 5 to gain the lead at the critical moment.

41. Unwilling Ally

My opponents on this hand from rubber bridge are capable players, my partner also a good player but belonging to the scientific school. With both sides vulnerable I pick up:

♠ A 7 6 2 ♡ K ◇ Q 9 7 ♣ K 8 6 5 3

My partner opens **one heart** and after a pass by East I respond **two clubs**. With the opponents remaining silent, partner raises to **three clubs**. I don't see much point in introducing three spades now, so I bid **3NT** and all pass. The bidding has gone:

South	West	North	East
—	—	1♡	pass
2♣	pass	3♣	pass
3NT	pass	pass	pass

West opens the Queen of hearts and partner displays this moderate holding:

♠ J 4
♡ A 9 7 3
◇ K 10 8 4
♣ A 7 4

♡ Q led

♠ A 7 6 2
♡ K
◇ Q 9 7
♣ K 8 6 5 3

"I like to open 1NT, but playing with you I have to bid one heart," observes my partner, quite unashamed. I certainly don't like these 12-point notrumps, either vulnerable or not. As dealer, vulnerable, it wouldn't occur to me to open this hand at all.

On the Queen of hearts East plays the 6 and I win with the King. If I give up a club and the clubs are 3 – 2 I'll have seven tricks on top but I may or may not have time to establish a trick in diamonds. In any event I shall probably need to find the Jack of diamonds to make nine tricks.

Suppose I play on diamonds first. If I find the Jack that will give me eight tricks on top, with some chance of making a ninth trick from hearts or from a squeeze.

At trick 2 I run the 9 of diamonds and lose to East's Jack. East switches to the 5 of spades. I play low and West wins with the Queen. West returns the 8 of spades and East plays the King on dummy's Jack. To have any chance now, I must assume that East has five spades and that West has the Ace of diamonds. I can't afford to give them another spade trick, so I win with the Ace.

Both opponents play low on the Queen of diamonds. When I lead a third diamond now, West goes up with the Ace and East discards the 3 of spades. West exits with a fourth diamond to dummy's King, East discards the 2 of clubs and I throw a spade. The position is now:

I have lost three tricks so far and if I can duck a club into West's hand I can probably make the remainder. Somehow I don't think that's going to be possible. That club discard by East is very sinister. I know that East began with five spades and two diamonds and I think that he also had four clubs and two hearts.

East played the 6 of hearts on the first trick and his second heart may well be the 8. That would explain why West did not continue hearts. He would know that after the play of the Jack, won by the Ace, dummy's 9 7 would be equals against the 10. Well then, what about leading the 9 of hearts from dummy? Yes, but not immediately. First I must lay down the Ace of clubs to remove West's exit card.

On the Ace of clubs East plays the 9 and West the 10. I continue with the 9 of hearts from dummy and East, as I was hoping, drops the 8. West wins with the Jack and returns a small heart. We are now down to four cards:

```
        ♠ —
        ♡ A 7
        ◇ —
        ♣ 7 4

        ♠ 7
        ♡ —
        ◇ —
        ♣ K 8 6
```

The finesse of the 7 of hearts wins and the Ace of hearts then squeezes East in spades and clubs, giving me my ninth trick. This was the full hand:

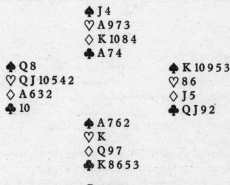

```
                    ♠ J 4
                    ♡ A 9 7 3
                    ◇ K 10 8 4
                    ♣ A 7 4

♠ Q 8                               ♠ K 10 9 5 3
♡ Q J 10 5 4 2                      ♡ 8 6
◇ A 6 3 2                           ◇ J 5
♣ 10                                ♣ Q J 9 2

                    ♠ A 7 6 2
                    ♡ K
                    ◇ Q 9 7
                    ♣ K 8 6 5 3
```

Post-mortem

Declarer had to base his play on the hope that the player with the Ace of diamonds would have a doubleton spade. On that assumption, which proved correct, it would have been a mistake to hold up twice in spades. Had the defence been allowed to win a second spade they could have defeated the contract in a number of ways.

Declarer's accurate card-reading in this hand deserves a little study. Note how the fall of the 6 of hearts from East at trick 1 suggested the possibility that his second heart would be the 8. Even without the indication, declarer would have had to play for that chance. Note, too, how declarer rightly read the club distribution. East's discard of a low club on the fourth round of diamonds strongly suggested that he had begun with at least four, as with 5 – 3 – 2 – 3 distribution he would surely have discarded a heart.

The general count of the hand showed that declarer had to cash the Ace of clubs before exiting with the 9 of hearts in order to force the heart return from West.

42. Unwanted Possession

My partner on this hand of rubber bridge is a player of notoriously poor judgment. It is therefore with some apprehension that I contemplate this indeterminate two-suiter:

♠ 6 4   ♡ K Q J 9 3   ◇ —   ♣ Q 10 8 6 5 4

We are vulnerable and my alarm is not lessened when West, on my left, deals and opens **three clubs.** My partner overcalls with **3NT** and East passes. In view of my club holding it is evident that the bid of 3NT is for a take-out. I bid a cautious **four hearts** and partner now introduces **five diamonds.**

I wonder whether I ought to pass before someone doubles. It would be a difficult decision with a good partner—quite impossible with a bad one. It may be foolish but I'm going to bid **five hearts.**

It *was* foolish. Partner's next move is **six diamonds** and now East **doubles.** I can only pass and prepare my apologies, but it's not all over. After many nervous glances over his spectacles, partner transfers to **six hearts.** East **doubles** almost in the same moment and all pass. The bidding has been:

South	West	North	East
—	3♣	3NT	pass
4♡	pass	5◇	pass
5♡	pass	6◇	double
pass	pass	6♡	double
pass	pass	pass	

West leads the King of clubs and partner's hand is in a way better than I was expecting:

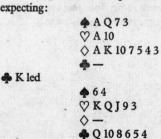

        ♠ A Q 7 3
        ♡ A 10
        ◇ A K 10 7 5 4 3
        ♣ —

♣ K led

        ♠ 6 4
        ♡ K Q J 9 3
        ◇ —
        ♣ Q 10 8 6 5 4

Digressing for a moment, I don't mind 3NT for a take-out over a major suit but over a minor it loses too much bidding space. To my mind, a better system is to play a double of three clubs or three diamonds as primarily for a take-out and a double of three spades or three hearts as primarily for penalties.

On North's present hand it is better to overcall three clubs with a cue-bid of four clubs. That suggests a more unbalanced type of hand. When on the next round North bids five diamonds over South's four hearts, it is easier for South to pass.

Exactly how I am going to play six hearts I don't know yet. At any rate, I must ruff the first club with the Ace of hearts. East follows suit, so I can take it that the clubs are 6 – 1.

Perhaps it's one of those hands on which one has to ruff one diamond and concede another. On the surface, if both red suits are not worse than 4 – 2 I can come to 12 tricks by way of five hearts, five diamonds, Ace of spades and a club ruff. But entries are a problem. I would like to give up the very first round of diamonds but I can't be sure of ducking the trick into East's hand. A spade lead from West would be very inconvenient. I am going to begin with Ace, King and another diamond and see what transpires.

Both opponents follow to the top diamonds and I discard two clubs. On a third diamond East plays the Queen. Is there any advantage in letting him hold this trick? Not really, because if the diamonds are 4 – 2 West will ruff his partner's trick and lead a spade. So I ruff the diamond with the 9 of hearts and, a little to my surprise, West follows with the Jack of diamonds.

That's good in one way but perhaps bad in another. If East has only four cards in the minors he may well have five hearts and four spades to the King. Furthermore, West is more likely to be 3 – 1 – 3 – 6 than 2 – 2 – 3 – 6. Can I do anything about it if East has five trumps? I think perhaps I can. One fortunate thing about this hand is that East, having a singleton club, is entirely cut off from his partner.

The position at the moment is as follows:

♠ A Q 7 3
♡ 10
♢ 10 7 5 4
♣ —

♠ 6 4
♡ K Q J 3
♢ —
♣ Q 10 8

If I draw trumps, and they are not 5 – 1, I make an overtrick with no difficulty at all. But life isn't like that. Besides, East is looking quite pleased with himself still. I can make the contract even if the hearts are 5 – 1, and that's what I'm going to assume.

I lead the 3 of hearts to dummy's 10. West follows, I am glad to see, for the hearts could have been 6 – 0 as well! Now comes the decisive moment. I play a winning diamond from dummy and East discards a spade, West a club. Better! East ruffs the next diamond and looks aggrieved when I leave him in possession of the trick. It is plain now that whether he leads a heart or a spade I can make the rest of the tricks. I show him my cards and he concedes the contract, the full hand being:

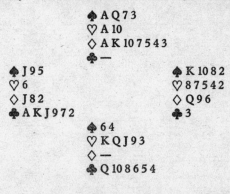

```
                ♠ A Q 7 3
                ♡ A 10
                ♢ A K 10 7 5 4 3
                ♣ —
♠ J 9 5                          ♠ K 10 8 2
♡ 6                             ♡ 8 7 5 4 2
♢ J 8 2                          ♢ Q 9 6
♣ A K J 9 7 2                     ♣ 3
                ♠ 6 4
                ♡ K Q J 9 3
                ♢ —
                ♣ Q 10 8 6 5 4
```

Post-mortem

Declarer's analysis of the distribution confirms a point that has been mentioned before. When opponents double one high contract after this sort of bidding sequence they generally have still better defence (or think they have) against the other. Six diamonds, as it happens, would have been a lay-down.

Had the diamonds proved to be 4 – 2 South would have had to cut his losses, taking care not to let West into the lead. The best continuation, after ruffing the third diamond, would have been to lead the top trumps and try to throw the lead to East on the fourth round.

43. Innocent Appearance

Playing in a pairs event against experienced opposition, I hold as dealer:

♠ 92 ♡ A Q J 9 5 ◇ K 8 ♣ K 7 6 3

We are vulnerable, the opponents not. I open **one heart,** West passes and my partner responds **one spade.** East intervenes with **two diamonds.** Rightly or wrongly, I bid **two hearts,** and partner raises to **four hearts.** The bidding has been:

South	West	North	East
1♡	pass	1♠	2◇
2♡	pass	4♡	pass
pass	pass		

West leads the 7 of diamonds and partner goes down with a useful hand:

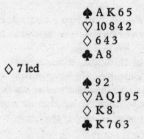

```
              ♠ A K 6 5
              ♡ 10 8 4 2
              ◇ 6 4 3
              ♣ A 8
◇ 7 led
              ♠ 9 2
              ♡ A Q J 9 5
              ◇ K 8
              ♣ K 7 6 3
```

East wins the first trick with the Ace of diamonds and returns the Queen. I cross to the King of spades and run the 8 of hearts. When this holds, I finesse the Queen and this time West discards a club.

Eleven tricks are certain, but at the moment I don't see any good play for a twelfth. If East had been short of hearts I would have ruffed two clubs, but now it seems certain that East will overruff. He overcalled in diamonds and has turned up with three hearts, so he is unlikely to have four clubs. In fact, West's discard of a club probably means that he has at least five. If I am not going to ruff clubs, I may as well play off the Ace of hearts. On this trick West discards a diamond and East's King falls. These are the remaining cards:

♠ A 6 5
♡ 10
♢ 6
♣ A 8

♠ 9
♡ J 9
♢ —
♣ K 7 6 3

Up to now I have not been thinking about West. If he has fourth round control of both black suits I should be able to bring some pressure to bear on him. Suppose I play a spade to the Ace and ruff a spade, then cross to the Ace of clubs and ruff a diamond? That's no good because I can't get back to dummy to play the 10 of hearts.

Another possibility is to play Ace and King of clubs, ruff a club in dummy, return to my hand with a diamond ruff and then play the last trump. But then West will discard a spade, relying on partner to guard that suit.

To exert real pressure on West, I must keep a trump in both hands. Suppose I cross to dummy with a club and immediately ruff a diamond? Yes, that's the answer.

When I cross to the Ace of clubs and return to hand by ruffing a diamond West is in obvious difficulties. He finally throws a club. Now I play King of clubs and ruff a club in dummy. After the Ace of spades a spade ruff puts me in hand to make the last club for a second overtrick. West was caught in a ruffing squeeze at the finish, the full hand being:

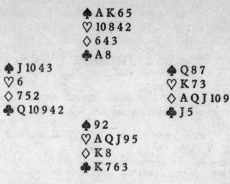

```
            ♠ A K 6 5
            ♡ 10 8 4 2
            ◇ 6 4 3
            ♣ A 8
♠ J 10 4 3                    ♠ Q 8 7
♡ 6                           ♡ K 7 3
◇ 7 5 2                       ◇ A Q J 10 9
♣ Q 10 9 4 2                  ♣ J 5
            ♠ 9 2
            ♡ A Q J 9 5
            ◇ K 8
            ♣ K 7 6 3
```

Post-mortem

This was the position after South had drawn the Ace of hearts:

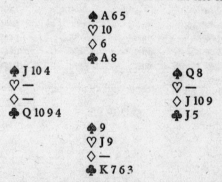

```
            ♠ A 6 5
            ♡ 10
            ◇ 6
            ♣ A 8
♠ J 10 4                      ♠ Q 8
♡ —                           ♡ —
◇ —                           ◇ J 10 9
♣ Q 10 9 4                    ♣ J 5
            ♠ 9
            ♡ J 9
            ◇ —
            ♣ K 7 6 3
```

The innocent-seeming diamond ruff was the only way to turn the screw on West. When both hands contain potential winners that may be established by ruffing, it is usually right to play for a position in which both dummy and declarer have one trump left.

44. Tempting Offer

Playing in a team-of-four match against opponents who are not particularly strong, I hold second in hand:

♠ K J 9 4　♡ J 6　◇ K 5 2　♣ A Q 10 2

Both sides are vulnerable and after a pass by East I open **one club**. Partner responds **one diamond** and I rebid **one spade**. Partner raises to **three spades**. There will probably be some finesses in this, but I must go to **four spades**. The bidding has been:

South	West	North	East
—	—	—	pass
1♣	pass	1◇	pass
1♠	pass	3♠	pass
4♠	pass	pass	pass

West opens the 4 of diamonds and a fair dummy goes down:

```
              ♠ Q 10 7 5
              ♡ A 4
              ◇ A 10 7 6 3
              ♣ J 4
◇ 4 led
              ♠ K J 9 4
              ♡ J 6
              ◇ K 5 2
              ♣ A Q 10 2
```

This lead looks like a singleton, but I can be grateful that they haven't led a heart. There are several ways of playing this. I can go up with Ace of diamonds and finesse a club. If it loses I can still dispose of the heart loser in dummy, but if East has the Ace of spades my King of diamonds may be ruffed. On the other hand, if I take the diamond in hand I have no convenient way of entering dummy for the club finesse. I can play a spade, but then they will knock out the Ace of hearts before I have touched clubs. Another possibility is to win in hand with the King of diamonds and lead a low club, abandoning the finesse. But then again I may run into diamond ruffs unnecessarily.

It is hard to assess all these chances, so I will follow the natural line of going up with the Ace of diamonds and finessing in clubs. East plays the 8 of diamonds under the Ace and covers the Jack of clubs with the King. Now I don't have to rush for the heart discard, so after winning with the Ace of clubs I lead the 9 of spades. This holds the trick and I follow with the 4 of spades to dummy's 10. Now a slight shock as East shows out, discarding the 7 of hearts! The contract has suddenly become difficult again. These are the remaining cards:

♠ Q 7
♡ A 4
◇ 10 7 6 3
♣ 4

♠ K J
♡ J 6
◇ K 5
♣ Q 10 2

I can discard a heart from dummy on the 10 of clubs and can take a ruff on the table in either hearts or clubs. But then I shall be in dummy and badly placed. If at that point I lead a diamond the King will be ruffed, West will draw the Ace of spades, and I shall still have a diamond and one other trick to lose. Alternatively, in the diagram position, I can play a trump, but then West will return a trump and again I shall be a trick short.

I wonder if I can do anything with the long diamond in dummy. Suppose I play a diamond right away. West will ruff, draw the Ace of spades and lead a heart. Then I shall be an entry short to make anything of the fifth diamond.

Still, that does give me an idea. It looks odd, but suppose I were to duck a diamond. If East has the King of hearts and not the K Q he may fall for the temptation of giving his partner a diamond ruff. Then, if my calculations are correct, I shall be a tempo ahead.

I'm going to try this because I don't think there's any other way of doing it. I play a diamond from dummy, East plays the 9 and I duck. West discards the 5 of hearts. East studies this for some while and then makes what seems to him the obvious play of a diamond to give West a ruff. West draws the Ace of spades and exits with a heart to dummy's Ace. Now the situation has improved:

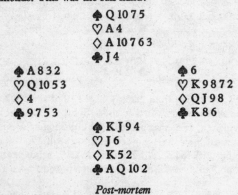

```
        ♠ Q
        ♡ 4
        ◇ 10 7
        ♣ 4

        ♠ K
        ♡ J
        ◇ —
        ♣ Q 10 2
```

I ruff a diamond with the King of spades, play the Queen and 10 of clubs, and make the last two tricks with dummy's Queen of spades and 10 of diamonds. This was the full hand:

```
                    ♠ Q 10 7 5
                    ♡ A 4
                    ◇ A 10 7 6 3
                    ♣ J 4

    ♠ A 8 3 2                       ♠ 6
    ♡ Q 10 5 3                      ♡ K 9 8 7 2
    ◇ 4                             ◇ Q J 9 8
    ♣ 9 7 5 3                       ♣ K 8 6

                    ♠ K J 9 4
                    ♡ J 6
                    ◇ K 5 2
                    ♣ A Q 10 2
```

Post-mortem

East did not defend well, but the situation was quite complex and many players would have done the same.

Declarer's stratagem of ducking a diamond when he was sure that the King would be ruffed is worth noting. A similar position sometimes arises in a side suit which is distributed as follows:

```
            10 x x x x
    x                       A Q J 9
            K x x
```

West leads his singleton. East wins with the Ace and returns the Queen. By playing low South gains a tempo which may help him to establish the long card in dummy.

142

45. The Little Old Ladies

The occasion, a big pairs tournament at a French resort; the opponents, two little old ladies whom I have never seen before. Both sides are vulnerable and I pick up as dealer:

♠ K Q J ♡ K J 10 ◊ K 10 6 2 ♣ A K 7

This 20-point hand with only one Ace is by no means ideal for **2NT**, but against the present opposition I will take the chance.

West passes and partner responds **three diamonds**. We have not arranged to play this as conventional in any sense, so I take it as constructive. Having opened sub-minimum, I mustn't force it. Even little old ladies can cash two Aces when they have them. I bid **3NT**.

Partner raises to **6NT**. That's enough for me. The full bidding:

South	West	North	East
2NT	pass	3◊	pass
3NT	pass	6NT	pass
pass	pass		

West opens the Jack of clubs and partner puts down:

♠ A 6 4
♡ A 7 5
◊ Q J 9 5 3
♣ 4 3

♣ J led

♠ K Q J
♡ K J 10
◊ K 10 6 2
♣ A K 7

East plays the 5 of clubs. I win with the King and force out the Ace of diamonds. A club comes back. Both follow to a second round of diamonds.

So I have to find the Queen of hearts, with no count and no indication of any kind. I could play off three more rounds of diamonds, but it is unlikely that would help.

One possibility is to lead the Jack of hearts in the hope of tempting a cover should West hold the Queen. But even little old ladies are unlikely to fall for that.

On the other hand, she may *hesitate* and then produce a small heart. . . .

But what would that mean? Unfortunately, I don't know her habits. Some of these little old ladies are very tricky: they hesitate when they haven't got Queens. On the other hand, she may hesitate and be quite honest, actually holding the Queen.

So I shall have to guess, unless. . . .

Yes, I have it! I'll lead the Jack of spades and see what this little old lady does when she does not hold the Queen.

On the Jack of spades, a tiny hesitation. I put on the Ace, return to hand with a diamond and lead the Jack of hearts.

No hesitation now, none whatever.

Finesse!

Successfully, for this is the full hand:

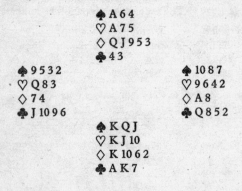

```
                    ♠ A 6 4
                    ♡ A 7 5
                    ◇ Q J 9 5 3
                    ♣ 4 3
  ♠ 9 5 3 2                        ♠ 10 8 7
  ♡ Q 8 3                          ♡ 9 6 4 2
  ◇ 7 4                            ◇ A 8
  ♣ J 10 9 6                       ♣ Q 8 5 2
                    ♠ K Q J
                    ♡ K J 10
                    ◇ K 10 6 2
                    ♣ A K 7
```

Post-mortem

In so far as this little fable has a moral, it is that it is foolish as well as (if done with conscious intent) unethical to form these revealing habits of play. I am thinking of West's hesitation when the Jack of spades was led.

There are many situations where, without any thought of deceiving, players give free indications. For example, when a defender to 3NT hovers from one lead to another before finally settling on an indeterminate 5, he tells the world that as likely as not he is leading from a short

144

suit. In a trump contract, when a defender leads after long thought you can dismiss the possibility of his having selected an obvious lead like a singleton.

The most difficult opponents are those who maintain an even tempo in both bidding and play. Of course, after a long sequence of bidding, the player on lead sometimes had to consider strategic possibilities, and that takes time. But when the bidding has been 1NT – 3NT, a player who hesitates over his lead is not deliberating, he is just dithering.

From the other side of the table, one should train oneself to observe these variations in behaviour and to draw the appropriate inferences, displaying what the French call "présence à la table".

One other point: if you think you have been diddled by an opponent's unethical play, don't claim a foul! Don't even betray any consciousness of what has happened. Like a poker player, just store the incident in your mind and resolve always to do the right thing in future against that particular opponent.

Book II

DEVELOP YOUR
BIDDING JUDGMENT

Foreword to the First Edition

Most players, in these days, have evolved a reasonable technique of constructive bidding which serves them for 75 per cent of all deals. In this book I aim to deal with the remaining 25 per cent where a player is out on his own and must use his judgment—where no textbook or point count will help him, and where bidding system has little bearing.

I have followed the over-the-shoulder technique which seemed popular in *Play Bridge with Reese*. The reader shares my thoughts at every stage of the bidding. Whether he agrees with my eventual answer is not so important—naturally there may be differences in bidding style that will affect the decision. The test is: Has some train of thought, some general principle, emerged from the discussion which will perhaps help to solve a later problem at the table?

The setting of the problems is given sometimes as rubber bridge, sometimes as a team event with international match-point scoring, sometimes as a match-pointed pairs tournament. The objectives at IMP scoring are broadly similar to those at rubber bridge. In a pairs event the bidding is keener in the sense that a player must strive to gain small advantages even at the risk of an occasional disaster.

It is assumed throughout that partner is a good player. True, one needs judgment to play with bad partners also, but what is right with one bad partner is apt to be wrong with another, so that general principles cannot be usefully extracted.

> *There is a demand nowadays for the*
> *man who can make wrong appear right.*
> —Publius Terentius Afer (190–159 B.C.)

PART ONE

Problems in Constructive Bidding

The sequence of hands in this book is not especially significant. Many could have been classified under more than one heading, and there is no reason why the reader should not dip in where he pleases.

The method of studying each individual problem could be important. My suggestion is that after noting the list of alternatives you think out the problem and, for choice, write down how you would mark the various calls. If, when you read on, you disagree with my answer and are not impressed by the argument, come back to the example in a week's time and see if it strikes you at all differently.

In this first group of questions the opponents may in some cases have entered the bidding, but the eventual decisions are not competitive. The problem is to find the best answer in a constructive sequence.

1. Long Memory

At rubber bridge, with our side vulnerable, I pick up a hand well outside my normal range in this form of contest:

♠ K 2　♡ A K 7 6 5　◇ A K 6　♣ A K 7

East deals and passes and I open **two clubs**, the big bid in our system. West passes and North bids **two diamonds**, the negative response. East **doubles** this, presumably on the strength of a diamond suit. I have three possible calls now. I could pass to see what my partner would say, I could bid 2NT, defining my general strength, or I could show my hearts. I was going to bid **two hearts** if East had not doubled two diamonds, and that seems the straightforward action now.

West introduces **three clubs** (with diamond support in reserve, I dare say), partner bids **three spades**, and East passes. The bidding so far:

South	West	North	East
—	—	—	pass
2♣	pass	2◇	double
2♡	3♣	3♠	pass
?			

It is a close decision now between four spades and 3NT. If partner has something like Q J 9 x x in spades with no sure entry we may be better off in the suit. However, he did call freely over three clubs and I feel that he should either have a six-card suit, in which case he can return to four spades, or some value in one of the other suits. So I bid **3NT**, West passes, and now North bids **four hearts**. East passes and I have to think again after the sequence:

South	West	North	East
—	—	—	pass
2♣	pass	2◇	double
2♡	3♣	3♠	pass
3NT	pass	4♡	pass
?			

In view of North's original two diamonds, it might be wrong to try for a slam. The most cautious advance would be to four spades, as this could be passed by North. More energetic slam tries would be five hearts, five spades, 4NT, or five of a minor. Even if we reject a leap to six hearts, which would certainly be too bold (though many would do it), the list of alternatives cannot be shortened from:

> Five Spades
> Five Hearts
> Five Diamonds
> Five Clubs
> 4NT
> Four Spades
> Pass

The Choice

Before examining the relative merits of 4NT and calls at the level of five, we must study whether any slam try is advisable.

Limits of North's hand

The requirements for a positive response to two clubs are not precise in terms of high cards, but I would expect partner to bid two spades with A Q 10 x x and a side Queen, and personally I wouldn't wait for the Queen. Having denied even such a modest holding, North will consider himself free, with a mindful partner, to do some bidding thereafter below the game level on quite moderate values. Let's look at a few specimen hands and see how they fit in with the sequence he has adopted:

> (1) ♠ A 9 x x x   ♡ Q x x   ◇ x   ♣ x x x x

This is the most North could have, and over 3NT a good player would have bid more than four hearts. He would bid five hearts or perhaps four diamonds. With this hand opposite, the slam would normally depend on hearts being 3 – 2.

> (2) ♠ Q 10 x x x x   ♡ J x x   ◇ x x x   ♣ x

Another possible holding for partner. He would take out 3NT because the hand should play for at least one extra trick in hearts. He knows South has a fair heart suit, for otherwise he would not have bid the suit when two diamonds was doubled. Here there is not much to choose between four hearts and four spades, but we would not want to be any higher.

$$(3) \spadesuit A x x x x x \quad \heartsuit J x x \quad \diamondsuit x x \quad \clubsuit x x$$

A maximum for partner but still the slam would be no lay-down, with the likelihood of uneven division in the minor suits.

$$(4) \spadesuit Q J 10 x x \quad \heartsuit Q x x x \quad \diamondsuit J x \quad \clubsuit x x$$

With heart support of this quality North would have given a clearer picture of his assets by jumping to four hearts on the second round.

$$(5) \spadesuit A x x x x \quad \heartsuit J 10 x \quad \diamondsuit x x \quad \clubsuit J x x$$

A likely hand, on which again we would be content to stay out of a slam.

The higher calls

It is clear from these examples that a slam is unlikely to be comfortable and that it may be dangerous to go beyond the level of four. The only advance that is at all safe is to four spades, which partner will not regard as forcing. Of the higher calls, five spades is more dangerous than the rest because it excludes five hearts, and 4NT is particularly inept. If intended to be natural, and capable of being passed, it may be too high. If it is a conventional bid, it will solve no problems. I mark the alternatives:

Pass	10
Four Spades	7
Five Hearts	3
Five Diamonds	3
Five Clubs	3
Five Spades	1
4NT	1

Reflections on the Bidding

One of the marks of a good bidder is that he remembers not only partner's last bid, but the one before that, and the one before that as well. This is a good example. It is easy to be distracted by the intervention and the number of bids that have been made, and to forget that partner is thinking all the time, "He knows I bid two diamonds to start with."

Another way for South to assess the situation is to reflect that he has a minimum two club opening and that not enough has happened to improve his hand. If partner had been able to bid one of the A K x suits, that would have given much better cause for optimism.

2. Rare Contribution

In a team event neither side is vulnerable and as dealer I hold:

♠ K J 63   ♡ A 3   ◇ K Q 10 2   ♣ 10 9 4

We are playing in theory a weak 1NT of 12 to 14 points. This hand of 13 points qualifies and I open 1NT. Any other opening would in fact present problems on the rebid. West overcalls with **two hearts** and my partner bids 2NT. East passes and the question is whether I should press on after the sequence:

South	West	North	East
1NT	2♡	2NT	pass
?			

The Alternatives

I can pass 2NT, raise to game, or make some exploratory bid at the three level. Some case could be made for three spades, three hearts or three diamonds. I have another suggestion which will appear later, but for the moment we may consider the alternatives to be:

3NT
Three Spades
Three Hearts
Three Diamonds
Pass

The Choice

As weak notrump hands go, this one containing 13 points plus two tens is by no means a minimum. Had there been no intervention I would not have hesitated to bid the game, for raises to 2NT are always based on the presumption that the opener will bid game unless dead minimum.

After the intervention I have to allow for various possibilities: that partner has stretched, that he has no heart stop (for that would not necessarily deter him from supporting notrumps in this sequence), and that the hand may play better in a suit which he has had to suppress.

After my 1NT and the two hearts by West he might reasonably bid 2NT on any of the following hands:

(1) ♠ Q 10 x x ♡ 10 x x ♢ A x x ♣ K Q x
(2) ♠ x x ♡ K x ♢ x x x x ♣ A Q J x x
(3) ♠ A x x ♡ Q x ♢ A x x x ♣ J x x x
(4) ♠ x x x ♡ J x ♢ J x x ♣ A K J x x

With a little luck we might make game in spades or notrumps on certain of these holdings, but I don't see any method of advance that would enable us consistently to find the right contract. The first conclusion that partner will draw if I introduce a suit at the three level is that I am nervous about the hearts, probably having no stop. Thus if I take out into three spades he will raise to four not only on hand (1), where we might make it, but also on hand (3), which would play better in notrumps.

The message of Three Hearts

Three hearts would be an uncommon bid in this sequence and I am not sure what he would make of it. I suppose it would say, "I hold the Ace of hearts but in case you have no guard yourself I am giving you a chance to bid three spades." The objection to transmitting that message is that too often, as on hand (4) above, partner would not be able to co-operate in either direction.

Three Diamonds slightly safer

If I am to make any call at the three level, three diamonds would give us the best chance of obtaining a plus score. With support for diamonds he could pass and on occasions he would be able to transfer to 3NT.

Prospects of game uncertain

Although I have enough in points to bid 3NT I have decided against that because my heart guard is the wrong type. West will open his long heart suit, and I have only the Ace. Besides, partner may have stretched. It is quite likely that he would have passed 1NT. I am not sure that any bid at the three level would improve our situation and I mark the alternatives:

Pass	10
Three Diamonds..	7
Three Hearts	6
Three Spades	5
3NT	5

Reflections on the Bidding

South was in an awkward position here, one that comes up quite often. I seldom make contributions to theory, holding that there are too many conventions already, but it does occur to me that when the responder to 1NT has been prevented by an overcall from employing the Stayman routine (two clubs asking for a four-card major) the opener should be able to initiate the conventional enquiry with three clubs.

That would be a good way out on the present hand. South bids three clubs over 2NT, asking partner to bid a fair suit of spades or diamonds, to bid 3NT if he has a suitable holding in hearts, or to pass if his best suit is clubs. This convention would be especially useful when the opener had no guard in the enemy suit.

Postscript

The modern tendency is to treat 2NT over intervention as purely competitive and not a try for game. My idea of using three clubs as "reverse Stayman" still seems good to me, though it has gained only limited acceptance.

3. Unusual Inference

In a pairs event, with both sides vulnerable, I hold as dealer:

♠ 8 2   ♡ 4   ◇ K Q 5   ♣ K J 10 9 7 6 3

At duplicate as well as at rubber bridge I like to make numerous and variable pre-empts and some say that when I catch sight of a seven-card suit I don't look at the rest of the hand. Well, this time I notice the clubs first and I open **three clubs**. The club suit is about minimum for a vulnerable three bid, but there is a trick outside and most players who use weak three bids in principle would accept this call. After a pass from West my partner responds **three hearts**. The opponents remain silent and I have to consider my rebid after the sequence:

South	West	North	East
3♣	pass	3♡	pass
?			

The Alternatives

The change of suit after a three bid is forcing, so a pass is excluded. The weakest call would be four clubs. If I want to co-operate in a game try I can bid four diamonds or bid the game direct in clubs or notrumps. The alternatives are:

> Five Clubs
> Four Clubs
> Four Diamonds
> 3NT

The Choice

Partner's change of suit over the three bid is unlimited and can cover a wide range of hands. He may be confident of game and thinking of slam in clubs. He may be intending to pass a sign-off of four clubs. He may be prepared for 3NT. He may be looking for game in hearts with a suit such as A Q J x x x which wants just a little support.

Too good to sign off

Obviously I cannot raise the hearts, but as I often make three bids on worse hands than this I prefer not to sign off in four clubs. A jump to five clubs seems unsuitable when the suit contains two losers and there is a K Q outside.

Four Diamonds preferable to Five Clubs

Four diamonds scores over five clubs in two respects. It is more informative should partner have his eye on a slam, and it still leaves room for us to play in four hearts.

3NT conveys a special inference

The remaining call, 3NT, has the virtue of retaining the option to play in any one of three game contracts. Against it, on the surface, is the fact that the clubs lack two high honours and there is a distinct weakness in spades.

As to the first of these objections, if partner reckons to make tricks from the clubs he will hold A x or better, so at worst we shall be fishing for the Queen.

The second objection—the weakness in spades—becomes less important if one can assume that partner will draw a neat inference. Had my spades and diamonds been reversed I would have bid three spades over three hearts, for this is a situation where the pre-emptive opener tries to show partner where his outside strength lies. When I bid 3NT over three hearts there is an inference that I am weak in spades. Compare these two possible North hands:

> (1) ♠ K 10 x   ♡ A K Q 10 x   ◇ J x   ♣ A x x
> (2) ♠ J x   ♡ A K Q 10 x   ◇ J 10 x x   ♣ A Q

On hand (1), since he holds the spades himself, he lets 3NT stand. On hand (2) he takes out 3NT into four clubs, which I pass.

If we meet disaster in 3NT because partner has overlooked this particular inference, I won't accept all the blame. This is the bid I select and I mark the alternatives:

3NT	10
Four Diamonds	7
Four Clubs	5
Five Clubs	3

Reflections on the Bidding

The main interest in this problem lay in the inference that North should draw about South's spade holding.

A similar situation often arises when a player bids 3NT in circumstances that suggest he is taking a chance on one suit. Suppose that South holds:

♠ K x x ♡ J x ◇ A Q J x x ♣ A 9 x

The bidding begins:

South	North
1◇	1♠
2♣	3◇
?	

South will probably bid 3NT now. There is then an inference that his weaker suit is hearts, for had his hearts and clubs been reversed, the bid over three diamonds would surely have been three hearts.

4. Working Well

My partner at rubber bridge is a capable player. Our side is vulnerable when I deal and pick up:

♠ A Q 10 7 5 4   ♡ Q 8 6 4   ◇ K   ♣ A 5

I open **one spade** and the opponent on my left overcalls with **two hearts**. My partner comes in with **three clubs** and East passes. I have to look for a satisfactory rebid after the sequence:

South	West	North	East
1♠	2♡	3♣	pass
?			

The Alternatives

The main choice is between a simple rebid in spades and a rebid more indicative of my strength. I could jump to four spades, I could raise the clubs, and 3NT is a possibility. Three hearts would be a way to extract some further information from partner. If we include that, the alternatives are:

Four Spades
Three Spades
Four Clubs
3NT
Three Hearts

The Choice

This problem solves itself for players who will say that as partner has come in at the three level he must have a goodish hand and will surely bid again over three spades. The effect of that argument is that one can never play in three spades. When partner has shown fair values in a competitive situation I must take that into account in choosing my next bid, not sit back and expect him to bid the same cards twice.

In other words, three spades on this far from minimum hand would throw a strain on a partner who had perhaps stretched a little to overcall in the first place.

Four spades is the obvious alternative, but it might not be the best game contract. My holding in hearts raises a doubt. Unless my partner has a singleton heart, I can foresee West's cashing his top hearts and then giving his partner a ruff. After that there might be another loser for us in spades or diamonds.

Four clubs is open to the same objection, that it might play unluckily after a heart lead. In any case five clubs will be better than four spades only when partner is very short in spades.

All cards working in notrumps

In 3NT the four hearts to the Queen will cease to be a liability. Tricks may come from either suit, spades or clubs. Playing in spades, I might be cut off from dummy's clubs and unable to dispose of my heart losers.

The singleton King of diamonds does not strike me as a serious drawback. West will hardly lead the Ace of diamonds even if he has it. Actually, the King of diamonds is likely to be a much more useful card in notrumps than in spades, whether partner holds the Ace or not.

Would Three Hearts solve any problems?

Yes, to the extent that it would enable us to choose more accurately between spades and clubs. Played according to the modern style, three hearts would not confirm clubs but would promise game values and request partner to declare himself further. With K x or J x x in spades he would show that support, with K x in hearts he would bid 3NT, and if unable to do either of those he would probably repeat his clubs.

Compare these two hands:

(1) ♠ x x   ♡ x x   ◇ A x x   ♣ K Q 10 x x x
(2) ♠ x   ♡ x x   ◇ A x x x   ♣ K Q 10 9 x x

On hand (1) he would respond four clubs to three hearts and would pass my next bid of four spades. On hand (2) he would go to five clubs over four spades, having drawn the inference that my spades were not solid.

Three hearts is an improvement on four spades, therefore, but too often it would lead to our by-passing 3NT, which, it will be observed, would be the best spot on either of the hands above. Judging 3NT to be the contract in which my hand will be most effective, I mark the alternatives:

3NT	10
Three Hearts	7
Four Spades	5
Three Spades	4
Four Clubs	3

Reflections on the Bidding

Questions of partnership understanding entered into this problem, but whatever one's interpretation of three spades or three hearts, the analysis ending in preference for 3NT is, I think, instructive. Apart from the spade suit itself, all the features of South's hand are designed for 3NT rather than four spades.

Many players would fail to consider 3NT because of the singleton King. There they miscalculate. For the most part—and especially when the main strength is on the declarer's left—a singleton King will play the same role as K x.

5. Providing the Tricks

At rubber bridge I deal and pick up:

♠ J ♡ A K 7 4 ◇ A 8 4 ♣ A Q 7 4 2

Neither side is vulnerable and I open **one club**. Partner respond, **one spade** and I reverse with **two hearts**. Partner repeats his suit, **two spades**. The question is how close we are to game after the sequence:

South	West	North	East
1♣	pass	1♠	pass
2♡	pass	2♠	pass
?			

The Alternatives

Partner's rebid is limited, and I could pass two spades. The obvious bids in the medium range are 2NT and three spades. I could try the effect of three diamonds or I could bid game from hand with 3NT or four spades. If the problem were put to several players their answers would cover this wide range:

Four Spades
Three Spades
3NT
2NT
Three Diamonds
Pass

The Choice

My reverse of two hearts promised a better than minimum hand but was not forcing after a response at the range of one. Partner has made about the weakest bid available. He might be no better than:

(1) ♠ A 10 8 x x x ♡ x x ◇ J x x ♣ x x

Now two spades would be quite high enough. That is sufficient to show that a jump to four spades or, still worse, 3NT would be unsound, but it does not follow that game hopes should be abandoned. North could have a more useful hand, such as:

(2) ♠ K Q 10 x x x   ♡ Q x   ◇ x x x   ♣ x x

Or:

(3) ♠ K 10 9 x x x   ♡ x x x   ◇ J x   ♣ K x

Four spades would be a good contract with either of these hands. [Some players would say that hand (1) was worth a jump to three spades over the reverse; it is close.]

There would similarly be a good play for 3NT if North held:

(4) ♠ A Q 10 x x   ♡ x x x   ◇ Q x x   ♣ 10 x

Because of the diamond position it would be better for North to be the declarer at notrumps. That is one argument for three diamonds or three spades on my hand in preference to 2NT. There are others. A bid of 2NT will give partner the impression that I am relying on my own hand for tricks at notrumps, rather than on his spades. On many hands he will bid 3NT when we would be better off in four spades.

What would Three Diamonds mean?

If one had a close understanding with partner concerning a bid of the fourth suit it might be possible to bid three diamonds as a request to him to make one more descriptive bid—either 3NT or a repeat of the spades or delayed support for one of the other suits. However, in rubber bridge the sequence would be a little ambiguous; partner might take it as a genuine suit and bid on the assumption that South was void of spades. Also, if North bid three spades over three diamonds, South would not know whether to bid the fourth.

Because of this uncertainty I judge three spades to be the best call. Some credit must be given to a pass, because sometimes eight tricks will be the limit. Any jump to game would be an overbid and also might land the partnership in the wrong game. I mark the alternatives:

Three Spades	10
Three Diamonds..	6
2NT	6
Pass	5
Four Spades	3
3NT	1

Experience has shown many times that when the player with the strong hand has a singleton of partner's long suit he should aim to play in the trump contract and not at notrumps.

It is true that when two poor bidders meet this kind of situation they surmount it successfully. The big hand bids notrumps and the weak hand invariably takes out into the long suit!

A standard example occurs when the bidding between two such partners begins three spades—3NT and always the first player goes back to four spades. Sometimes 3NT will be the right contract and players who bid in this style can never stop there.

When the bidding between two good players goes:

South	North
1♣	1♠
2♡	2♠
3NT	

South's 3NT says one of two things, either:

"I have enough strength in spades to bring in your suit."

Or:

"I have a strong suit of my own and expect to make nine tricks without the use of your spades. Don't take me back!"

6. A New Look

In a pairs event I note that a rather stolid-looking couple have come to our table. While I am thinking about this and that, I see that, with no one vulnerable, I have to speak first on:

♠ K J ♡ A 5 ◇ K 9 8 6 2 ♣ 10 7 4 3

Disdaining the customary gambit to the effect that I didn't realize it was my deal, I open, guiltily, **one diamond**. West overcalls with **one heart**, my partner bids **one spade**, and a raise to **two hearts** by East happily relieves me of the necessity to find a rebid. However, I am not off the hook for long. After two passes my partner reopens with a jump to **four diamonds**, and I have to take another look at my hand after this sequence:

South	West	North	East
1◇	1♡	1♠	2♡
pass	pass	4◇	pass
?			

The Alternatives

Partner's jump is not altogether forcing, so having opened light I am free to pass. Since my few high cards may be well placed, I can play for game in either four spades or five diamonds. By bidding four hearts I might perhaps induce partner to choose between those two contracts. The alternatives are:

Five Diamonds
Four Spades
Four Hearts
Pass

The Choice

At most tables, it is charitable to assume, South will have passed originally. My opening bid may have turned out luckily. If four diamonds, scoring 130 or 150, is going to be a good result, I don't need to improve on it.

West probably hasn't got an opening bid, but North, holding a spade suit and enough for a double jump in diamonds, probably has. If West and I had passed, he surely would have opened with one spade. What would have happened then? I would have responded two diamonds, he would presumably have raised to three, and I would have tried three spades. Thus I cannot take the comfortable view that we already have a good score owing to my irregular opening.

The hand has improved

I might pass for a different reason—that I had opened sub-minimum and had no excuse for bidding again unless forced to. That is a shallow sort of argument. Revaluing my hand as the bidding progresses, I conclude that all my 11 points are fully operational. The 13 or 14 points of many a sound opening dwindle to 6 or 7 working points after a round or two of bidding, but my assets, such as they are, have increased in worth.

Game in spades or diamonds?

This I find difficult to judge. Partner is more likely to have five spades than six, for with six he might have preferred three spades on the second round. He must have high cards as well as distribution, for otherwise the opponents would not have subsided at two hearts. Let's look at some possible hands he might hold:

$$(1) \spadesuit A Q x x x \quad \heartsuit x x \quad \diamondsuit A J x x \quad \clubsuit J x$$

Not much to choose between the game at spades or diamonds. We cannot afford to lose a diamond in either contract.

$$(2) \spadesuit A x x x x \quad \heartsuit x x x \quad \diamondsuit Q J x x \quad \clubsuit A$$

This might be grisly in four spades, but five diamonds would be fairly safe. Perhaps he wouldn't let four spades stand.

$$(3) \spadesuit A Q x x \quad \heartsuit x x \quad \diamondsuit Q J 9 x \quad \clubsuit A 10 x$$

Now he would certainly transfer four spades to five diamonds, remembering that I did not raise to two spades on the previous round. Four spades will also be the more popular contract because of the match-point factor, and if only for that reason I ought not to go beyond it.

Is Four Hearts a solution?

Four Hearts would be cute if partner could be relied on to take it as a request to choose between four spades and five diamonds. The objection is that he might read it as a slam try, my hand having been greatly improved by the raise in diamonds. I am not so much concerned about his carrying me to six diamonds (which might even make!) as about his by-passing four spades. It might not occur to him to repeat anything less than a six-card suit.

I conclude with regret that four hearts would not be entirely sound, and I mark the alternatives:

Four Spades	10
Five Diamonds	7
Four Hearts	7
Pass	4

Reflections on the Bidding

The choice between the three bids at the finish was close and the main interest of the hand lies in South's decision not to pass. This was reached in two stages. First, he had to work out that although his unsound opening seemed to have turned out well, other pairs might be in game. Second, he had to forget that his opening bid was sub-minimum and revalue his hand in the light of later developments.

7. Encouraging Sign

In a team event I am third to speak and hold:

♠ 5   ♡ J 9 8 6 3 2   ◇ K 8   ♣ A Q 10 4

Neither side is vulnerable and my partner opens **one diamond**. East, on my right, overcalls with **one spade** and I come in with **two hearts**. West raises his partner to **two spades**, my partner bids **three diamonds**, and East passes. The question is which way to move after the sequence:

South	West	North	East
—	—	1◇	1♠
2♡	2♠	3◇	pass
?			

The Alternatives

Any game bid would be excessive, but I could test partner's reaction to four diamonds or four clubs. If I judge game in diamonds to be remote, I can repeat my hearts or pass. The remaining possibility is three spades—an attempt to manœuvre partner into 3NT if he can control the spades. That makes five calls to be considered:

> Four Diamonds
> Four Clubs
> Three Spades
> Three Hearts
> Pass

The Choice

The intervention by both opponents has deprived us of bidding space and I cannot tell whether partner would have made a jump rebid had we been left to ourselves. Probably not, but he must be better than minimum to rebid freely at the three level. He won't have less than:

(1) ♠ J x   ♡ Q x   ◇ A Q J 9 x x   ♣ K x x

The fact that he has not supported my hearts is, in its way, an encouraging sign. If he has a singleton heart the fit in diamonds will be that much better. There would be a good chance for five diamonds if he held no more than:

(2) ♠ x x x ♡ K ◇ A Q 10 9 x x ♣ K J x

The prospects for game are surely good enough to justify a further call.

Three Hearts

The bid that appeals least is three hearts. Partner cannot go on bidding his own hand forever and if he has a singleton heart he may have to pass. That is one of the few ways in which we could end up with a minus score. Failure to rebid hearts now does not, of course, exclude the possibility of our reaching four hearts.

Four Diamonds

One of the merits of this bid is that it gives partner a good opportunity to show secondary support for hearts. Four diamonds also seems about right on values and the information about the King of diamonds may be what North most needs to know. So far, I see no objection to this call.

Four Clubs

The information that I have values in clubs would probably be more useful to my partner if he knew about my King of diamonds. Otherwise, I feel that we shall be battling in the dark. If over four clubs he bids four hearts or five clubs, I shall be uncertain whether or not to transfer to five diamonds; and if he bids four diamonds, I shall have no idea whether or not to raise. In that sense four clubs is a trap bid.

Three Spades

The main purpose of this call would be to extract 3NT from partner if he held this sort of hand:

(3) ♠ Q J x ♡ 10 x ◇ A Q J 10 x x ♣ K x

Now 3NT is the only game we can make. However, I feel that this is a long shot and the bid is open to the same objection as four clubs—that if it produces a bid of four diamonds from North, I shall be no further on.

Summing up

To bid three spades or four clubs now and follow with five diamonds would make my hand sound stronger than it is. (For example, if four clubs were raised to five and I then bid five diamonds, partner might conclude that I was angling for six.) It occurs to me that a direct raise to five diamonds would be as good as some of the calls we have been looking at. Putting the interloper in brackets, I mark the alternatives:

Four Diamonds	10
Three Spades	6
Four Clubs	5
(Five Diamonds	5)
Three Hearts	3
Pass	3

Reflections on the Bidding

This was a fairly straightforward exercise in constructive bidding, but two general points emerge.

First, there was the expectation of a good fit in diamonds arising from partner's temporary denial of hearts. When it looks as though partner may have a singleton of your Jack-high suit, that is an indication that his high cards in other suits will fit well with yours. By contrast, a holding such as K Q x x x x in a suit where partner may be short is a bad sign.

Second, the objection raised against the bids of three spades and four clubs is, I think, instructive. South knows that the partnership is close to five diamonds, and the way to obtain co-operation from partner is to tell him so by raising the diamonds—not to make an uninformative call that may force him to bid four diamonds and still leave you none the wiser.

The same principle often arises for the defending side. With both sides vulnerable, an opponent opens one club and you overcall one spade, holding:

♠ A Q 8 6 4   ♡ J 6   ◇ A 10 9 6 3   ♣ 4

Partner bids two hearts. Now if there is game at all it is likely to be in four hearts and you should raise to three. It is a mistake to bid three diamonds and then not know what to do when partner repeats his hearts.

8. A Slam Philosophy

Playing in a team event, with neither side vulnerable, I hold as dealer:

♠ A Q J   ♡ K 9 2   ◇ A J 6 3 2   ♣ J 6

I open **one diamond** and partner responds one heart. That gives me a slightly awkward rebid. A simple raise to two hearts would suggest, in our system, not much better than a minimum opening, and here I have 16 points in high cards plus a ruffing value and a five-card suit. The hand is actually midway between two hearts and three hearts. The best measure for the moment may be to temporize with **one spade**. This elicits **3NT** from partner, which I take to show about 13 to 15 points. The question is whether I should try for a slam after the sequence:

South	West	North	East
1◇	pass	1♡	pass
1♠	pass	3NT	pass
?			

The Alternatives

I could let the bidding rest at 3NT. Four hearts is a possibility and so is 4NT (natural, not conventional). I could bid four diamonds to see what that would produce. A more direct slam suggestion would be five hearts. I wouldn't consider anything higher than that, so the alternatives are:

Five Hearts
Four Hearts
4NT (natural)
Four Diamonds
Pass

The Choice

Partner's minimum is a hand just too good for a non-forcing 2NT and his maximum is a hand just short of a force. This could be 15 or a moderate 16 (counting high cards alone). It is clear that if he is not much better than minimum there will be no play for a slam, and a game contract such as 3NT or four hearts will be enough. If he is maximum and fits well, there could be a slam. Six hearts would be a fair venture if he had either of these hands:

(1) ♠ 10 x x ♡ A Q x x x ◇ K x ♣ A Q x
(2) ♠ x x ♡ A 10 x x x x ◇ K ♣ A Q 10 x

What I have to decide is whether there is a safe way of approaching any slam there may be. I don't want to languish at the five level, or even the four level, and then go down!

Without stopping to construct possible hands that my partner may hold, I know that 4NT, with a combined 29 or 30 points, would be no certainty against a bad break. In addition, the heart support in my hand is likely to be an important element in any slam, so any try that concealed that support would be unsatisfactory.

Would Four Hearts be a slam try?

That's a point I haven't discussed directly with my present partner, but it seems uncertain. Take a hand of this type:

♠ A Q x x ♡ J x x ◇ A Q x x x ♣ x

After the same bidding sequence of one diamond—one heart—one spade—3NT, four hearts would be the natural bid on this far weaker hand.

A second question is whether four hearts would always be safe. It could fail if there were two losers in the trump suit and other finesses went wrong.

Would Four Diamonds lead anywhere?

Unlikely. If partner bid four hearts or five diamonds I still wouldn't be confident about going any higher.

The answer to the hand seems to be that it is difficult to find a slam try that will not be too forceful and will at the same time convey the heart support. Since four hearts would not be a clear slam try and might not be so safe a contract as 3NT, I mark the alternatives:

Pass	10
Four Hearts	8
4NT	4
Four Diamonds	4
Five Hearts	2

Different systems would tackle this hand in a different and perhaps more satisfactory way. It happens to be an awkward hand for my system, the way the bidding has gone, and the value of the example lies in the mental approach toward the possibility of making a slam try.

Analysis of match records almost always shows more points lost than won by attempts to reach borderline slams. That is because players move too quickly to the question, "What slam try shall I make?" They forget to ask themselves first whether any slam try is safe and whether, if they reach a slam, they can be reasonably sure of playing in the right suit.

No partnership is good enough to bid all the slams that come its way. The sensible policy is to bid the obvious ones and let the rest escape.

Postscript

The reader may think that I have been unduly critical of a raise to 4NT. Of course, ten tricks will be there more often than not, but consider these two hands in partnership:

♠ A Q J	♠ K 9 5
♡ K 9 2	♡ Q 8 6 4 3
◇ A J 6 3 2	◇ Q 4
♣ J 6	♣ A K 7

Responder is full value for his 3NT, but he wouldn't be too happy in 4NT against a club lead. I might have made more of the point that, with 7 points wrapped up in ♠ A Q J, the South hand is less powerful than it may seem at first.

PART TWO

Doubles—Competitive, Co-operative and Crass!

In the following group of hands the question of whether to double (or accept partner's double) comes strongly into consideration. It is a department of the game where even top-notch players sometimes fail badly in their judgment. In the examples dealing with close doubles I draw attention to questions that are often overlooked, such as:

Does my hand contain any unpleasant surprise for the declarer?

Can I form a clear picture of how the defence is likely to go?

If the double is in any sense co-operative, has my partner sufficient information on which to decide intelligently whether to let the double stand?

Must I risk the double (in a match-pointed event) in order to have a chance of a good score?

9. Never Return

With both sides vulnerable in a keenly fought rubber, I deal and hold this awkward hand:

♠ — ♡ Q J 8 7 ◇ J 8 6 5 2 ♣ A K Q 4

There are three possible opening bids, and it might even be a good idea to pass and judge later what action to take.

The call I find easiest to reject is one heart. The hand is not strong enough to bid as a three-suiter and I am prepared to let the hearts go unless partner can mention them.

As between one diamond and one club, there could be advantage in calling the suit where the top cards are, but sometimes it works the other way. Moreover, a sequence such as one club—one spade would be difficult to handle.

After thinking so long I can't very well pass, so **one diamond** it is. The opponent on my left bids **three spades**, my partner **doubles**, and the next hand passes. Does that suit me or not, the bidding having gone:

South	West	North	East
1◇	3♠	double	pass
?			

The Alternatives

If I take the double out, the obvious bid is four clubs, but 3NT is also a possibility. Four hearts would sound too strong, so the alternatives are:

Four Clubs
3NT
Pass

The Choice

The void in spades is no reason for taking out a double at this level. I am worried more by the indifferent quality of my diamond suit. An opening lead of the King of diamonds from K x would certainly be an unhappy start to the defence.

On the surface, I should be regretting that I opened one diamond and not one club, but there is another way of looking at it. If I had opened one club partner might have counted on tricks from a diamond holding of his own such as A K 10 x. It is always a shock to open a short suit that has not been bid and see the first lead ruffed.

My hand contains defensive values in hearts and clubs and for all I know partner may have several tricks in spades. The suit could be divided 8 – 4 – 1 – 0, or something of that sort. I have no reason to despair of our chances of beating three spades, but before I decide to leave the double I must consider whether there is a satisfactory take-out.

The rescue bids

I don't suppose we would go far wrong in four clubs. If partner is short of diamonds he should have at least three clubs and possibly more. The suit could break badly against us, though.

3NT would be a wild venture. Where would the tricks come from? It is not as though I had a long and solid suit anywhere.

Who can tell?

Defending against three spades doubled may be our best spot. The fact is that from my side of the table I cannot tell. Partner, on the other hand, may be entirely confident, and for that reason I think it is sensible to accept his decision. If I rescue into a losing contract when we could have set them 800, he won't be interested in my explanations. I am going to pass and I mark the alternatives:

Pass	10
Four Clubs	6
3NT	2

Reflections on the Bidding

When you are doubtful about leaving in a double, lack of a high honour in the suit you have bid is a disadvantage, certainly, but one that players tend to exaggerate. Often partner has a low singleton, and the lead does no active harm. What *is* dangerous is possession of a long unbid suit headed by the Jack or 10. Partner often has A K x̄ x or A K Q alone of this suit, and the expected tricks tend to disappear.

As to the psychological aspect, I cannot express this better than the Dutch player, Herman Filarski, when the problem was put to him:

"*Pass.* Because I remember West hands with seven or eight spades and North with A K 10 8 x. Take out such a double and you never can go back to that club again. Three spades doubled and made is a smaller risk and, moreover, you can say: 'Partner, you should not have doubled.'"

10. They Lose Weight

Playing in a team-of-four match I hold in third position:

♠ J 8   ♡ K Q 10 7   ♢ 9 6   ♣ K J 10 5 3

We are vulnerable and my partner opens **one spade**. East overcalls with **two hearts**, which I am happy to **double**. West takes out into **three diamonds**, North passes and so does East. The question is what further move can I make, the bidding having gone:

South	West	North	East
—	—	1♠	2♡
double	3◇	pass	pass
?			

The Alternatives

I can pass or double. If I bid on, it will have to be three spades or four clubs, or perhaps three hearts, with the idea of extracting a further bid from partner. If we include that, the alternatives become:

Four Clubs
Three Spades
Three Hearts
double
Pass

The Choice

Let's begin by disposing of the idea that three hearts is a practical possibility. Following a penalty double of two hearts, it could be taken as a genuine suit, such as A Q 10 x x x. I can't risk that, vulnerable.

Now what conclusions can we draw about North's hand? Probably two or three small hearts, for East is likely to have six and West a void or singleton.

North won't have much in diamonds, either in length or strength. If he had either, he would have doubled three diamonds.

As he is short in both red suits, it is safe to assume that he has five spades and he may well have six. He would not rush in with three spades because I might be short and might be waiting to double three diamonds. As to clubs, he will have at least two, and possibly three or four. These are some possible holdings:

(1) ♠ A Q x x x x ♡ x x ◇ K x ♣ Q x x
(2) ♠ A K 10 x x ♡ J x ◇ A x ♣ x x x x
(3) ♠ K Q 9 x x x ♡ x x x ◇ J x ♣ A Q

One point that is immediately obvious is that opponents might well make three diamonds. It would be quite unsound to double.

What about four clubs? Probably one down, possibly more. The obvious danger is that opponents will begin with Ace of hearts and a heart ruff and then cash two diamonds unless North has the Ace. If North has the King, as in hand (1), it may well be under the Ace.

With the hands shown above, three spades will also go down more often than not. Of course, North could be stronger. Suppose that he held:

(4) ♠ A K 10 x x x ♡ x x ◇ x x ♣ A Q x

Now there would be a fair chance of three spades, and three diamonds would be a make for the other side. The trouble here is that North, expecting more, would bid four spades and go down.

Time to go quietly

We are left with a pass, which may seem timid opposite an opening bid but at the vulnerability is probably the right course. Maybe they will make 130 when we could have lost 100 in three spades, but that is not serious. We don't want to lose 200—still less to double them out in three diamonds. This is how I mark the alternatives:

Pass	10
Three Spades	6
Four Clubs .. .. .. ∴	4
Double	1
Three Hearts	0

Reflections on the Bidding

This is a situation where a player's better judgment might tell him that he had no sound bid except a pass, but not all players would respond to their better judgment.

There is a type of player who would add up his ten points, plus two 10's, decide that opponents could not make nine tricks, and double. As we have seen, that is likely to be disastrous. It should be evident that the heart honours are not going to pull any weight in defence.

The objection to three spades is more subtle. We might have enough to make three spades, but when that is the case partner will almost surely bid four. If, as partners do, he says in the post-mortem, "Why didn't you bid three spades? We could have made that," the answer is that you could not have stopped there.

11. The Net

In a team-of-four match my opponents are vulnerable and East, on my right, deals and opens **one spade**. My hand is:

♠ A Q 10 6 2   ♡ K 7 6   ◇ 8 6 5   ♣ 6 4

I pass, awaiting better things. West passes and my partner **doubles**. Better things on the way! East passes and so do I. West attempts a rescue action with **1NT**. Partner passes and East transfers to **two diamonds**. I have to decide whether they have escaped our net after the sequence:

South	West	North	East
—	—	—	1♠
pass	pass	double	pass
pass	1NT	pass	2◇
?			

The Alternatives

If prepared to defend against two diamonds, I can double or pass the bid up to my partner. I can compete with two spades, the suit bid on my right, or possibly with two hearts, as partner is likely to have some length in the suit. The alternatives are:

Two Spades
Two Hearts
Double
Pass

The Choice

The bidding has been fairly informative. My partner has doubled in the protective position but he cannot be particularly strong or he would have doubled West's 1NT after my penalty pass. West is obviously weak, with a singleton or void in spades. East could have five spades and five diamonds but as he passed over the double he is more likely to be 5 – 4 or 6 – 4. Also, there is hardly room for him to hold five diamonds. My partner, for his take-out double, is likely to hold three diamonds. West, who took out one spade doubled into 1NT, will surely hold three or four diamonds, and I have three. So, the odds are that the suit is 4 – 3 – 3 – 3 round the table.

How will the hand play in diamonds?

For East, badly. If he tries to ruff spades in dummy he will be soon overruffed by my partner (the fact that I have no diamond honours is a good sign). If he draws trumps he will have several spades to dispose of. Our side must hold enough cards in clubs and hearts to prevent declarer from making many tricks in those suits.

Against two diamonds doubled I plan to lead a club rather than a trump, for I anticipate that partner's trumps will be useful for overruffing the dummy in spades. Partner will return clubs and declarer will soon have to ruff in front of my 8 6 5 of diamonds.

Partner is not bound to leave the double in if he is weaker in defence than his bidding so far has suggested. For example, if he has only a doubleton diamond he can take out into two hearts or even two spades —remembering that I was anxious to defend against one spade.

The other calls

As between two spades and two hearts, I would be on safer ground with two spades. If I had to guess, I would say that we would average to make eight tricks in spades. We might do better or worse in hearts, depending on the division of the suit. Partner can bid hearts if I pass, and since I expect to score at least 100 points if we defend against two diamonds undoubled, a pass must be judged better than two spades or two hearts. I think it would be unenterprising not to double, however, and I mark the alternatives:

Double	10
Pass	6
Two Spades..	4
Two Hearts	2

Reflections on the Bidding

This situation arose in a Gold Cup final and the double brought in no less than 800 points! North had Q 10 x of diamonds over the dummy's J x x and declarer lost a trick in the play because he did not expect the trumps to be 3 – 3.

I seldom recommend doubles at a low level without a trump trick, but this was an occasion where it was possible to arrive at a full and satisfactory answer to the important question, "How will the play go?"

12. Often in Danger

In match play, with neither side vulnerable, I hold in third position:

♠ 1085 ♡ A J 76 ◇ J ♣ A 9 7 5 3

My partner, sitting North, opens **one spade**, East passes, and I respond **two clubs**. West intervenes with **two hearts** and this is passed to me. The bidding has gone:

South	West	North	East
—	—	1♠	pass
2♣	2♡	pass	pass
?			

The Alternatives

The main choice lies between doubling the hearts and supporting the spades. If I decide to support the spades there may be a question whether I should raise to two or to three.

If I had held a doubleton spade and J x of diamonds I might have chosen 2NT to make some use of my heart honours, but with three spades and a singleton diamond that would be somewhat eccentric. I don't think we need look further than the three alternatives mentioned above:

    Three Spades
    Two Spades
    Double

The Choice

On the surface, all I know about partner's holding is that he has opened one spade and did not deem his hand worthy of a free rebid over two hearts. He is no doubt short of hearts and cannot have much in the way of club support.

There is no bar in our system to opening bids on a four-card major, but there is a strong inference here that partner has five spades. For one thing, he must have been prepared for a two heart response, and over that his rebid would presumably have been two spades. Another

187

way of arriving at the same conclusion is to reflect that he probably holds nine cards in spades and diamonds.

Two Spades or Three Spades?

If West had passed and North had rebid his spades, I would have had a *very* sound raise to three spades. That is sufficient to establish that two spades would be an underbid now and that I am worth three despite holding only three trumps.

What are the prospects of a double?

Certainly we will not make 500; however, if even 300 were likely, it would not be wrong to go for that in preference to an uncertain game.

Many players regularly double in this sort of position, observing rather loosely, "Partner can take it out if he doesn't like it." Even on that basis the double here is much too close for my liking. I see the following objections to it in principle:

(1) I have support for my partner's suit, which I have not shown. If partner has only five spades he will expect them to produce tricks in defence, and they may not.

(2) I don't see a clear-cut line of defence. Partner may well start off with an unfortunate lead such as Queen of clubs from Q x.

(3) My hand does not hold any unpleasant surprise for the declarer. He knows he is missing A J of hearts and was prepared to find them on the wrong side as well. As to my singleton diamond, that may well be duplicated by honours in partner's hand. If declarer's diamonds are someting like A x x he will be counting on two losers in any event.

(4) This is not the sort of situation that can turn up in a pairs tournament where one has to make a close double because there is no other way of obtaining a fair result. Probably we *can* beat two hearts by one trick, but we can score 140 or 170 with much less strain in two spades.

However, as I have said, I consider the hand worth three spades, and I mark the alternatives:

Three Spades	10
Two Spades..	5
Double	2

Reflections on the Bidding

When partner has been freed from the obligation to rebid, it is often helpful to reflect on what he would have called if there had been no intervention. Here, that line of thought led clearly to the conclusion that he must have intended to rebid his spades.

Of the arguments advanced against a double of two hearts, that of paragraph (3) is the one that "busy" players constantly overlook. It is a form of arrogance to double an opponent who has come in freely without taking into account that the bid presumably appeared sound to him when he made it.

I speak with some feeling on this matter because the fortunes of my team have been endangered on countless occasions by unsuccessful doubles of part-score contracts at the other table. The apologia usually begins along these lines: "How could I tell that the spades would be 5 – 0?" Or, still more infuriating, "The double was all right. If I had opened a diamond and my partner had underled his Ace of hearts . . ." Idiotic remark! If it needed a tough defence to beat them, the double was *not* all right!

13. The Right Conditions

In a match-pointed pairs tournament, with neither side vulnerable, I hold as dealer:

♠ A K 7 3 2   ♡ J 10 5   ◊ Q 6   ♣ 10 6 4

This is not the sort of hand on which I like to open, whether vulnerable or not, so I pass. West passes and my partner opens **one diamond**. I respond **one spade** and now West comes in with **two clubs**. This is passed to me and I have to contest in some way after the sequence:

South	West	North	East
pass	pass	1◊	pass
1♠	2♣	pass	pass
?			

The Alternatives

There does not seem much likelihood of game at the moment, but I can compete for the part score with either two spades or two diamonds. As we seem to have the majority of the high cards, we might get a good result from doubling two clubs. Any jump bid on my hand would be excessive in view of partner's pass on the second round, so the alternatives are:

Two Spades
Two Diamonds
Double

The Choice

If partner has a genuine opening we should be able to make at least eight tricks or so in spades or diamonds, and if he is a bit light in high cards he will have a fair diamond suit and we can probably make two diamonds.

Two spades would score better than two diamonds, but a disadvantage of bidding two spades is that we can't go back to diamonds. At worst, partner might hold:

(1) ♠ x ♡ K x x x ◇ A J 10 x x ♣ A x x

Now two spades could play very awkwardly.

On the other hand, if I bid two diamonds we can still play in two spades. With the match-point situation in mind, partner will bid two spades not only when he has three spades and four diamonds, but also with:

(2) ♠ 10 x x ♡ A Q x ◇ A J x x x ♣ x x

A Double co-operative

Two diamonds, then, is more flexible than two spades, but a double leaves the widest choice of all. I have less in clubs than I would like but my hand is nevertheless maximum in defensive values, considering that I passed originally. West also passed to begin with, and his hand is likely to consist of A Q J or K Q J six times in clubs with perhaps a side King and 6 – 4 – 2 – 1 or 6 – 3 – 3 – 1 distribution. He will expect to find something in the dummy, but may be disappointed. Or rather, he will be disappointed if my partner has the sort of hand on which he can pass the double.

Partner will not assume that my double, made in front of the club bidder, is based on strong trumps. Clearly he will be happy to pass on hand (1) above. On hand (2) he will remove to two spades. He will accept the double only when he has fair defensive values and not more than two spades.

It is true that one down doubled will not be as good as making two spades or three diamonds, but the difference will be small, and these doubles often bring in 300. I mark the alternatives:

Double   10
Two Diamonds 6
Two Spades.. 5

Reflections on the Bidding

On most occasions in this book I bear down on marginal doubles in the part-score area, so I include this example to show that I don't object to a snap double when the conditions are right. These are factors that make the double sound policy:

Partner will know that the double is not based primarily on trump tricks, for I am under the bidder and West must have a good suit.

If he doesn't like the double, he will have no problem about taking it out. He has the choice of two spades or two diamonds, and possibly even two hearts.

If he does pass the double, he will presumably lead a spade and the defence will be off on the right foot.

PART THREE

Tactical Moves

In this section, various tactical manœuvres are discussed. Among them are ways of escaping from a threatening penalty double, preparing a defence in a competitive auction, and tactical underbids in certain sequences.

14. Lines of Retreat

At rubber bridge my side is a game ahead when I pick up in third position:

♠ 4 ♡ Q 7 3 ♢ J 8 7 5 2 ♣ 10 6 4 3

My partner opens **one spade**, East passes, and I have no two thoughts about doing likewise. West reopens with a **double**, my partner passes, and so does East. I have to decide whether to start any rescue operations after the sequence:

South	West	North	East
—	—	1♠	pass
pass	double	pass	pass
?			

The Alternatives

There are four ways of attempting to improve the situation. I can redouble, bid 1NT, or take out into one of the minor suits. It could also be right to let the double stand, so the alternatives are:

Two Diamonds
Two Clubs
1NT
Redouble
Pass

The Choice

Partners who open one spade on a hand that is not particularly strong usually have a five-card suit. Also, had North been weak in spades he could have bid 1NT after West's double, with the intention, if necessary, of redoubling for a rescue. Thus, I don't expect to find him with a suit like A K x x. However, he could hold a fair five-card suit and still have a very awkward journey. A pass could not be criticized, but I am playing for points, not praise, and my instinct is to look for a more promising contract.

If the choice were between passing and rescuing into one of the minors, I would pass, but better techniques are available. Thus, 1NT would inform partner that I disliked the notion of one spade doubled and held scattered strength in the other suits. I wouldn't classify this necessarily as an "unusual no trump" showing length in the minors, but if partner had four cards in either minor he would surely take out 1NT.

Tactical advantage of Redouble

A redouble would surely be SOS, because I passed originally and also because if I were satisfied with the double of one spade I would leave it in.

Like 1NT, redouble gives us the chance to play in a second suit of partner's choosing, and it has the important advantage that it makes it possible to play 1NT from partner's side, without the prospect of a spade lead through the strength. A further point, perhaps a small one, is that if partner happens to be strong he can pass the redouble and let East do the worrying. By redoubling I at least prevent partner from saying afterwards: "Why couldn't you leave it in? I had seven (eight, nine?) tricks in my own hand . . ."

The minor suits

To rescue directly into either minor suit would be a mistake—if only because we would by-pass 1NT. Also, we could end in the wrong suit. To select two diamonds might be calamitous. Two clubs is slightly better, because if it is firmly doubled a retreat to diamonds is still possible.

The arguments for a redouble put it clearly ahead of the other forms of rescue, and I mark the alternatives:

Redouble	10
Pass	7
1NT	6
Two Clubs	3
Two Diamonds	1

Reflections on the Bidding

Two diamonds was the worst, and redouble the best, of the rescue manœuvres because two diamonds left open the fewest lines of retreat, redouble the greatest number. That is a line of thought worth bearing in mind for many situations where the future seems hazardous or obscure.

15. Out of Fashion

At rubber bridge both sides are vulnerable, and as dealer I pick up:

♠ A K 10 7 6 2   ♡ 4   ◇ K Q 9 6 3   ♣ 5

I open **one spade** and West overcalls with **two hearts**. My partner raises to **two spades** and East bids **three hearts**. I am faced with a familiar tactical problem after the sequence:

South	West	North	East
1♠	2♡	2♠	3♡
?			

The Alternatives

I can jump directly to four spades or approach that end more deviously by way of three spades or even a pass. Four diamonds must also be considered. Thus, the alternatives are:

   Four Spades
   Three Spades
   Four Diamonds
   Pass

The Choice

My objective is clear enough: I want to play in four spades, which I can probably make. I do not want to contend with five hearts if I can help it.

It is usual to suppress the second suit in this situation and to employ one of the three well-known stratagems. There is something to be said for each of them.

Four Spades

This is the straightforward call and it has the merit of raising the auction to a level at which it may be difficult for either opponent to overcall.

Three Spades

The object of this tactical underbid is to persuade the opponents that you are stretching when later you go to four spades over four hearts, assuming that the opportunity arises. The stratagem is well known and a further disadvantage—as compared with four spades—is that the opponents have more room in which to assess their potentialities. Moreover, opponents will sometimes refrain from disturbing three spades because they are fearful of having to compete against four spades.

Pass

This is a more subtle way of achieving the same kind of result, but it also requires more nerve. I shall look foolish if the opponents buy the contract for three hearts when we have eleven tricks in spades! However, since I have only 12 points, the odds are that someone else will bid. Either West will go to four hearts or my partner will persist with three spades. In either case, my eventual bid of four spades will be underestimated and may even be doubled.

Four Diamonds

There remains the unfashionable call of four diamonds. The advantage of exposing my two-suiter to all who choose to believe in it is that I go far to solving the problem that may arise at the level of five.

Suppose that we get to four spades by fast or slow stages and that the opponents inconveniently persist to five hearts. Even if partner doubles in front of me I shall be tempted to go to five spades. I shall not have to make this guess if I have bid four diamonds on the way. As an example, compare these two hands for partner:

(1) ♠ J 9 x x ♡ x x ◇ A J x x ♣ J 10 x
(2) ♠ Q 9 x x ♡ x x x ◇ x x ♣ K Q 10 x

On hand (1) he will go to five spades and on (2) he will double. Either way, I shall be content to let him decide.

Summing up

I would admire anyone who had the nerve to pass, but since the object of the problem is to point out the merit of Four Diamonds I mark the alternatives:

Four Diamonds	10
Pass	8
Four Spades	6
Three Spades	4

I think there is a general tendency to overlook the advantage of bidding second suits during a competitive auction. Suppose. that South holds:

$$\spadesuit x \quad \heartsuit KQJxxx \quad \diamondsuit xx \quad \clubsuit AQJx$$

The bidding goes:

South	West	North	East
1♡	1♠	3♡	3♠
?			

Now what is wrong with bidding four clubs ? It will stop a club lead, you say, against four hearts ? But you weren't expecting that anyway! What it *will* do is help your partner make an intelligent decision if they go to four spades.

16. Minority Vote

Playing in a pairs event against opponents of average standard, I hold as dealer:

♠ A 3　♡ A 9 8 6 5 4　◇ 7　♣ A 6 3 2

Both sides are vulnerable and I open **one heart**. West overcalls with **one spade** and my partner raises to **two hearts**. East now comes in with **three diamonds** and I have a problem in tactics after the sequence:

South	West	North	East
1♡	1♠	2♡	3◇
?			

The Alternatives

Three hearts or four hearts would be straightforward. Among the tactical possibilities are four diamonds, four clubs, and a pass. If we consider nothing more eccentric than these, the alternatives are:

Four Hearts
Three Hearts
Four Diamonds
Four Clubs
Pass

The Choice

We must have a play for four hearts and, unless partner is trickless, we should have a defence against four spades. Thus, the general objective is to play in four hearts or, if they defend, to extract the maximum penalty.

Not the moment for an underbid

I don't see this as a borderline competitive hand on which we might make four hearts and they four spades. On hands like that (as we noted in example 15) it may be good tactics to underbid, partly to deceive the opponents and partly to judge more accurately where the balance of strength lies. Here, they have so far not even agreed on spades, and if I jump to the level of four they may not get together—assuming, that is, that they have a fit at all. If I pass or bid just three hearts, I give West the opportunity to rebid spades and East will probably be able to go to four spades.

Preparing a defence

The best way, then, to attain our first objective—being allowed to play in four hearts—is to bid at the four level. The second objective is to prepare the best defence against four spades. That means taking our ruff in diamonds. If partner leads a heart against four spades doubled I can win with the Ace (I hope) and return my diamond, but there may be no subsequent entry to his hand that will enable him to give me the diamond ruff.

One possibility is to bid four clubs. Then I can take the club lead, return a diamond, and perhaps later put partner in with the King of hearts.

But why not four diamonds? That looks better still. For one thing, partner's entry may be in clubs, not hearts. For another, releasing the Ace of clubs may make it possible for West to discard a diamond on dummy's clubs.

When I win the first round of trumps, it shouldn't be difficult to decide where partner's entry lies. He may think of making a suit preference signal when he makes the opening lead of a diamond. If he does not, and I cannot see from the table which suit to return, I can lay down the Ace of clubs and note whether he gives me an encouraging signal.

I don't see any disadvantage in the four diamond call. A partner who has raised to two hearts and probably lacks an Ace is unlikely to carry me beyond four hearts. It fits in with both the original plans and I mark the alternatives:

Four Diamonds	10
Four Clubs	7
Four Hearts	6
Three Hearts	3
Pass	3

Reflections on the Bidding

In the original deal from which this problem was taken, North-South had to score the diamond ruff to defeat four spades by just one trick.

The problem was set in the *Bridge World* and the editor castigated his expert panel when only one out of fifty-eight voted for four diamonds. A few mentioned the bid but did not follow it up. I don't know why. It seems to me a good bid which I would be happy to find at the table.

17. A Little Rope

In a pairs event, with neither side vulnerable, my partner opens **one diamond** and the next player passes. My hand is:

♠ K J 9 6 2 ♡ — ◇ 9 7 5 ♣ K 10 8 6 2

I respond **one spade** and, after a pass by West, partner rebids **two diamonds**. East passes, and I have a rebid problem after the sequence:

South	West	North	East
—	—	1◇	pass
1♣	pass	2◇	pass
?			

The Alternatives

A pass of two diamonds is a possibility and so is a raise to three. I could repeat the spades or make a forward move in clubs. That makes the alternatives:

> Three Diamonds
> Three Clubs
> Two Spades
> Pass

The Choice

The next call has to be considered from two angles: Is the hand worth another bid, in that a pass may lead to a missed game? Even if game is unlikely, is it advisable to make another bid for tactical and defensive reasons?

Is it likely that we can make a game?

I doubt whether we can make more than nine or ten tricks in diamonds. Since nothing has been heard of the hearts it is likely that partner has four, but it does not follow that my hand will provide three ruffs. There may be duplication and there may be difficulty with entries. As soon as the defenders come in they will lead a trump, if they have not done so originally.

Game may be on, it is true, if partner has a void or a singleton Ace in one of the black suits. I could bid three diamonds without much risk of going too high. That would certainly be a better bid than two spades, suggesting a much better suit, or than three clubs, which would be forcing and would invite 3NT.

Is it necessary to bid for tactical reasons?

This is a more important question, because even if I pass two diamonds now I shall probably have another chance. Partner's strength is limited by his simple rebid and opponents presumably have nine or ten hearts between them. No doubt West is the stronger hand, for East had a chance to come in over one diamond. It is highly probable that if I pass two diamonds West will reopen with a double or two hearts.

Do I really want to prevent that by making a mild pre-empt such as three diamonds? I have an idea that if opponents find their fit in hearts they may have cause to regret it! Quite a likely type of hand for partner is:

♠ x ♡ K Q 9 x ◇ A Q J x x x ♣ J x

Two hearts he will pass, and if they reach four we will collect a good penalty.

If West bids two hearts and partner doubles at once I shall take out into three diamonds. If partner bids three diamonds himself, over two hearts, I will go to four diamonds over three hearts. Any such development seems satisfactory.

Resorting to *cliché*, this seems a moment where, if allowed a little rope, the opponents may hang themselves. I mark the alternatives:

Pass	10
Three Diamonds..	6
Three Clubs	2
Two Spades..	1

Reflections on the Bidding

The principle that emerges from this hand is that there is no need to prevent opponents from getting together when, if they do so, they will run into bad distribution. It is not when you have a void or a singleton, but when you have x x or x x x, that you may have to take defensive measures.

Suppose that after the same bidding by North-South, one diamond
—one spade—two diamonds, South had held:

♠ A x x x x   ♡ x x   ◇ K J x   ♣ x x x

There won't be a game anywhere and South is not worth a raise on
his values, but now there is a tactical case for three diamonds.

The same sort of argument applies to opening pre-emptive bids.
Compare these two hands:

(1) ♠ x x   ♡ A Q J 10 x x x   ◇ 10 x x   ♣ x
(2) ♠ —   ♡ A Q 9 8 x x x   ◇ 10 9 8 x x   ♣ x

On hand (1) you should pre-empt as high as you dare in relation to
vulnerability and position at the table. On hand (2) you can afford to
sit back and listen to the others.

PART FOUR

Making Progress after an Intervening Bid

In most of the examples in this section an intervening bid has created a problem. Sometimes the difficulty is simply lack of bidding space, at other times opposition bidding makes the choice of contract a delicate matter.

18. As Opportunity Offers

My partner at rubber bridge plays a sound game without any flights of fancy. I deal and pick up:

♠ A 4   ♡ 7 5 2   ◇ K 8   ♣ A Q 10 7 5 3

Neither side is vulnerable and I open **one club**. This is doubled on my left, partner **redoubles**, and East passes. If I bid two clubs partner will assume that I have a weak opening, so I pass and West bids **one heart**. Partner bids **two clubs** and East passes. The bidding has gone:

South	West	North	East
1♣	double	redouble	pass
pass	1♡	2♣	pass
?			

The Alternatives

There could be various opinions about the next move, ranging from a pass to a force of two hearts or a gambling 3NT. Three clubs would be a popular choice and we must also look at four clubs and 2NT. The best call should be somewhere among the following:

Four Clubs
Three Clubs
3NT
2NT
Pass
Two Hearts

The Choice

Partner's general strength can be estimated within fairly close limits. His redouble, in preference to 1NT or a jump in clubs, was an expression of confidence that we hold the balance of the cards. The odds are against his having a heart stop, for with a guarded King or Queen he might have preferred 1NT on the second round. Any of the following hands would be consistent with his bidding:

(1) ♠ Q 10 x ♡ x x ◇ A 10 x x ♣ K x x x
(2) ♠ K x x x ♡ 10 x x ◇ A x ♣ K x x x
(3) ♠ Q x x x ♡ A x ◇ Q x ♣ J 9 x x x

It is clear from these examples that there can be no question of passing on my hand. We would not be far from game on any of them.

Game in what? Well, 3NT would be a good proposition with (2) or (3) and by no means impossible on (1). West's one heart was in a sense forced, and he may well have only a four-card suit. East could hold four hearts but not enough general strength to raise.

Thus, a jump to 3NT comes well into the picture. The danger is a singleton heart opposite. Partner may hold something like:

(4) ♠ Q x x x ♡ x ◇ A x x x ♣ K x x x

I can avoid landing in 3NT opposite that hand by forcing with two hearts. That will extract a bid of 2NT (or three hearts) from him on hand (3), and on hand (4) we should find our way to five clubs. However, two hearts will not work out well when partner has no guard in hearts, for then we shall miss 3NT unless I bid it myself on the next round. If I intend to do that I might as well bid 3NT at once, with the psychological advantage that the defence may be discouraged from leading hearts.

It is this last consideration that inclines me to 3NT rather than 2NT. Partner will generally raise 2NT to Three, but the impression of a heart stop in my hand will be stronger when I bid 3NT myself.

Three and Four Clubs

Three clubs, though better than pass, would sound too defensive. With nothing in reserve after his redouble, North would often pass. The disadvantage of four clubs is that it goes beyond the likely game in 3NT.

Summing up

Two hearts would not be in any sense a mistake at this point. In a match it would be the right call, though South would have to take a further decision on the next round should partner sign off in three clubs. At rubber bridge 3NT strikes me as a good gamble and I mark the alternatives:

3NT	10
Two Hearts	7
2NT	7
Three Clubs	4
Four Clubs	4
Pass	1

Reflections on the Bidding

When this situation occurred at the table South bid a watery three clubs. "Offensive-defensive" action is what he called it. But who wants to be defensive in this sequence? The clubs appear to be solid and partner has redoubled, so game in 3NT should be lay-down unless the opponents can run five hearts tricks.

Why was it suggested that in a match South should make the safer call of two hearts? Because in a match the first objective should be to avoid action that may lead to an adverse swing. At rubber bridge, and also in a pairs tournament, a player must seize chances as they arise.

19. A Liability

With both sides vulnerable in a pairs event, the dealer on my right passes and in second position I hold:

♠ J 10   ♡ A K 9 5   ◇ J 9 7 6 2   ♣ 8 4

I pass and West opens **one diamond**. My partner overcalls with **one spade** and East passes. I have to find a call to reflect my modest values after the sequence:

South	West	North	East
—	—	—	pass
pass	1◇	1♠	pass
?			

The Alternatives

The most aggressive action I can contemplate is two hearts, the least aggressive is a pass. The natural bids in between are 1NT or two spades. That seems to cover the field:

Two Spades
Two Hearts
1NT
Pass

The Choice

This is probably a part-score hand, but if anyone can make game it is more likely to be our side than theirs. Four spades, 3NT and even four hearts are all within reach if partner's overcall is close to a maximum. On those grounds alone we can rule out a pass.

Whose hand is it?

This question asks, "If both sides do the best they can, who will end up with a plus score?" Supposing here that our maximum is eight tricks in spades, is it likely that they can outbid us, presumably in clubs?

There is no certainty about this, but we hold the majors and East did not bid on the first round. It is more likely to be our hand than theirs, but they could, of course, have a good fit in clubs.

The reason for considering a theoretical point of this sort is to judge whether a tactical rather than a descriptive bid is called for. If I thought that we were likely to be outbid on the hand I might incline toward a bid such as two spades. This would raise the level of the auction and might prevent the opponents from getting together. I intend to make what I think is the accurate call, however, as I do not particularly fear competition.

Two Hearts an exaggeration

There are obvious objections to two hearts. The suit is weak, hearts are not a likely spot for the two hands, and once I make this encouraging call I have shot my bolt and cannot do any more bidding. The best that can be said for two hearts is that it tells partner where my high cards are.

1NT or Two Spades?

The choice surely lies between these two and I can find many more arguments for 1NT than for two spades. Most important of these is that the diamonds should pull plenty of weight at notrumps but their length may be a liability in spades. If we play in three or four spades I can foresee a diamond lead and ruff, West put in with a club, another diamond lead, and so on.

It is slightly unorthodox to bid 1NT with a small doubleton in a side suit, but at this level it won't matter greatly if the opponents run the first five tricks in clubs. There will be some rubbish to be put in the basket while this goes on.

One might say too that it would be unorthodox to support the spades on a doubleton. In a general way I am not nervous about supporting an overcall on J 10, but there seems no tactical reason to do so here. As we noted, the hand may play badly in spades, and this is not the moment to raise on minimum trumps.

Finally, when there is a choice of calls I think it is a sound principle to choose the one that leaves the bidder with something in reserve. Thus, if I bid 1NT now I have some breath left and can bid two spades over two clubs. Similarly, if partner jumps to three spades over 1NT I can give him four without stretching. Players who follow the principle of keeping a bit in reserve seldom have to let their partners "hang" one trick short of game.

I have shown where my preference lies and I mark the alternatives:

1NT	10
Two Spades..	6
Two Hearts	3
Pass	3

Reflections on the Bidding

This is one of those problems where the average player is more likely to agree with my answer of 1NT than the more advanced player, who in these competitive positions tends to prefer the more obstructive bid of two spades.

Nevertheless, I am inclined to say that the expert who votes for two spades is guilty of lazy thinking. Remember the main points I have stressed here. There is no need to be obstructive, the diamonds will help in notrumps but not in spades, and the hand may in fact play badly in spades.

20. Untimely Intervention

Playing in a team-of-four match with IMP scoring, I hold as dealer:

♠ A J 7 5 3   ♡ A K J   ◇ 6 3 2   ♣ A 7

Our side is vulnerable and I open **one spade**. Partner responds **two clubs** and East intervenes with **three diamonds**. It is not going to be easy to find an accurate bid after the sequence:

South	West	North	East
1♠	pass	2♣	3◇
?			

The Alternatives

One way to ensure progress is to bid the enemy suit. Such rebids as three spades, three hearts, and four clubs must come into consideration. A pass would be well chosen if partner could be relied on to bid again. A double would bring in points more often than not. The alternatives are certainly numerous:

> Four Diamonds
> Four Clubs
> Three Spades
> Three Hearts
> Double
> Pass

The Choice

This pre-empt by the non-vulnerable opponent is probably based on seven top diamonds, but it may also be just a nuisance bid on K Q J 10 x x x and some distributional quirk. If so, it has achieved its object. Opposite partner's response at the level of Two I have the values to expect a game, but now I lack space in which to explore the right denomination.

Had East intervened with two diamonds I would have had two reasonable bids open to me: three diamonds, asking partner to bid 3NT or describe his hand in some other way, and two hearts. This last bid would be irregular, but I would have some room in which to escape from a game contract with inadequate trumps. We might begin by studying the effect of these bids at the higher level to which we have been pushed.

Four Diamonds

A cue-bid of the opponent's suit, with 3NT already behind us, would be taken as confirming clubs and promising at least second-round control of diamonds. We might land on our feet in five clubs but all future bidding would be guesswork.

Three Hearts

This might pass off all right. There would be no problem if partner bid three spades or four clubs. Less welcome would be a raise to four hearts. I would either have to try to make it, with the prospect of dummy's four trumps being forced immediately, or transfer to five clubs. Nor can I ignore the possibility that partner might take it into his head to pass three hearts.

Pass

That cannot be right, for it is quite likely that partner will be unable to continue. He will place the opponents with some of the Aces I hold.

Double

This would have to be considered at rubber bridge, where to accept a probable 300 in place of a problematical game is never wrong. At IMP scoring, to take 300 in place of a vulnerable game, not to mention a slam, costs several points and the chance of game here is too good to pass up.

Three Spades

Such overstatement of the spade strength could be disastrous, as this suit may be strongly held by West. It cannot be right to play in spades until partner has volunteered support.

Four Clubs

The trump support is well below normal for what in effect is a double raise, but that may be only a technical objection. Partner is likely to have one of two types of hand, of which the first will contain a long club suit, such as:

(1) ♠ Q x ♡ x x x ◇ x x ♣ K Q J x x x

Some players are forbidden by their system to respond at the level of two on such a hand, but my present partner is not of those. Having stretched already he would pass four clubs (and also three hearts, with less success!).

With a better hand of this type North will advance to five clubs or, if stronger still, make a cue-bid in diamonds.

The other type of hand is:

(2) ♠ K 10 x ♡ Q x x x ◇ x x ♣ K Q x x

When the clubs are moderate, as in this example, he will have secondary support for spades.

If one is going to make an irregular call, the objections to four clubs are less than those to three hearts, and I mark the alternatives:

Four Clubs	10
Three Hearts	8
Double	5
Four Diamonds	5
Pass	2
Three Spades	1

Reflections on the Bidding

When this situation arose at the table, North had a freakish 1 – 5 – 0 – 7 hand, with Q 10 x x x of hearts and K Q J 10 x x x of clubs. A grand slam could have been made in either suit and almost any bid would have led to six.

South's problem over three diamonds was difficult and at the time I thought his actual choice, three hearts, was the best. Closer study inclined me to four clubs, for the reasons given above. The situation is analogous to that when partner has made a defensive overcall and it becomes apparent from the bidding that all he can have is a strong suit. Having reached that conclusion one sometimes raises on a low doubleton and some tricks outside. On the present occasion the odds were that partner held good clubs—there wasn't room for anything else. That being so, the raise in clubs came clearly into the picture.

21. The Defence is Tricky

In a team event, with IMP scoring, our side is vulnerable and in fourth position I hold:

♠ Q J 9 7 4 ♡ Q J 6 3 ◇ J 7 3 ♣ 5

West, on my left, opens **1NT**. They are playing a weak 1NT when not vulnerable, about 12 to 14 points. My partner **doubles** and East passes. I have a difficult call after this short sequence:

South	West	North	East
—	1NT	double	pass
?			

The Alternatives

I can pass the double and probably collect a small penalty, or I can try for a vulnerable game. There are two agressive bids—three spades or 2NT, which would be conventional and forcing. Two spades would be a safe compromise. The alternatives are:

Three Spades
Two Spades
2NT
Pass

The Choice

Although the opponents are playing a weak notrump, my partner is in an exposed position and I expect him to hold upward of 15 points. We surely have the balance of the cards and, barring accidents, should be able to defeat 1NT. At rubber bridge it wouldn't be wrong to accept a penalty of 300, but at duplicate that would be a poor exchange for a vulnerable game. Also, it may be difficult to play the right defence against 1NT doubled. Partner will have to lead from strength, he won't know about my spade suit, and if we lose an early tempo declarer may make tricks in clubs. Actually, I never like passing 1NT doubled at this score unless my hand is weak and balanced.

Chances of game

After an opponent has opened 1NT, it is easier to play the hand than to defend. The position of the cards is marked, the strong defender has to make the leads, and 3NT can often be made on two or three points less than the standard 24 to 25. Similarly, if partner has support for spades, game in that suit should not present any problem.

Three Spades or 2NT?

There are two ways of approaching game. 2NT in this position is a conventional force, for with a moderate balanced hand I would pass the double. Partner will bid his best suit and then I can show my spades, leaving him to choose the final contract.

The alternative is a direct jump to three spades. Since 2NT is available as a forcing take-out, the jump in a suit should be non-forcing, in my opinion. The only objection to it is that partner might take me for a more distributional hand, such as:

♠ Q 10 x x x x ♡ x ◇ K x x x ♣ x x

Three spades would be right on that sort of hand, where I would want to be in game unless partner had a singleton spade. If I make that bid on the present hand we may play in three or four spades when 3NT would be better.

Two Spades too conservative

A simple take-out into two spades would guarantee a five-card suit, it is true, as with only four-card suits I would choose the lowest so as to give partner more room. However, two spades would not promise anything in high cards and partner would seldom be able to continue. If I am not going to play for the vulnerable game I may as well pass and hope for 300 or more.

Since I am optimistic about the chances of game, I mark the alternatives:

2NT	10
Three Spades	8
Pass	5
Two Spades..	4

Reflections on the Bidding

Responding to a double of 1NT is often tricky because partner cannot be relied on to have support for any particular suit. The points that have emerged from this discussion are:

When playing against a 12 – 14 no trump, it is too dangerous in North's position to intervene on a hand of similar strength. Unless he holds a good suit, his minimum for a double should be about 15 points.

In South's position at this score it seldom pays on an unbalanced hand to pass the double for penalties. The defence is apt to go astray and sometimes declarer has a concealed suit and makes 1NT doubled with much less than half the total honour strength.

On responding hands where there is a choice of contracts, 2NT is a valuable first move. It asks partner to bid his best suit and makes it possible to explore in more than one direction.

22. Deterrent Factor

At rubber bridge the vulnerable opponent on my right deals and passes. My hand is:

♠ Q 8 4   ♡ A K 8   ◇ Q J 10   ♣ K Q 10 4

As I am too strong for 1NT not vulnerable, I open **one club**. West overcalls with one diamond and partner bids **one spade**. East passes and I have a rebid problem after this sequence:

South	West	North	East
—	—	—	pass
1♣	1◇	1♠	pass
?			

The Alternatives

In terms of general value the hand is worth 2NT. Other bids of about the same strength are three spades or a reverse of two hearts. If I regard West's overcall of one diamond as a deterrent factor, I can hold back with 1NT or two spades. Two diamonds, as a general force asking partner to declare himself further, is another possibility. If we include that, the alternatives are:

Three Spades
Two Spades
2NT
1NT
Two Hearts
Two Diamonds

The Choice

The normal rebid in our system on a balanced 17 points is 2NT, but after West's overcall that seems unattractive. West would not have come in vulnerable after his partner had passed unless he had a good suit and some tricks. After a diamond lead, unless my partner can contribute a second stop, we shall have to run nine tricks straight off. There are many hands on which partner would bid 3NT where we would go down two, losing five diamonds and an Ace. And if partner had to pass 2NT, I would not expect to make it.

A bid of the enemy suit

Two diamonds, using a bid of the enemy suit as a general force, would ask partner to describe his hand further. It would be agreeable if partner were able to show a diamond stop by bidding 2NT, but unless that happened the manœuvre would take us no further. For example, if partner were now to bid three clubs or two spades I would have no idea whether to continue. Theoretically, I ought not to pass short of game.

The other strong calls

What of two hearts? Having shown a good hand by the reverse, I would be free to pass two spades, but either three hearts or three clubs would be embarrassing.

A jump to three spades would be an overbid by any standards—the more so with the prospect of a diamond lead and continuation.

Two Spades or 1NT?

I am going to choose one of the more conservative bids, but I haven't made up my mind yet as between two spades and 1NT. The distribution suggests notrumps, but in view of the diamond overcall game in spades is perhaps more likely. I am thinking of this sort of responding hand:

$$\spadesuit K J 10 x x \quad \heartsuit J x x \quad \diamondsuit x x \quad \clubsuit A x x$$

With such a dummy there would be no play for 3NT but we would have a good chance for four spades.

Two spades is slightly more encouraging than 1NT, and it does not exclude our playing in notrumps. If over two spades partner can muster three spades or three clubs, I can bid 3NT. He will leave that if he has three small diamonds or, unexpectedly, a diamond honour. As a matter of fact, when one constructs possible holdings for partner it becomes evident that two spades is scarcely an underbid. Finally, if partner is weak, 1NT can fail more easily than two spades for we might lose the King of spades, five diamonds and the Ace of clubs. I mark the alternatives:

Two Spades..	..	..	..	..	..	..	..	10
1NT	..	..	..	..	..	..	..	7
Two Hearts	..	..	..	..	..	..	..	5
Two Diamonds ..	..	..	..	..	..	..		4
2NT	..	..	..	..	..	..	..	4
Three Spades	..	..	..	..	..	..		2

Reflections on the Bidding

The problem illustrates that when there is a long suit against you the normal standard of 25 points for 3NT has no meaning. What you want, in addition to a guard, is a long suit of your own and *Aces*. Suppose that in the present example the opposite hand had been:

♠ A K J x x ♡ 10 x x ♢ x x ♣ J x x

Now the spades are good for five tricks, but to make 3NT after a diamond lead you want Ace of clubs instead of the combined K Q J.

23. Avoiding Ambiguity

In a team event both sides are vulnerable and in fourth position I hold:

♠ 7 6 2   ♡ A 7   ◇ A 9 5 4 2   ♣ A 6 3

After two passes East, on my right, opens **one diamond**. I pass, and West responds **two clubs**. Partner now enters with a **double**. East passes and I have to reassess my hand after the sequence:

South	West	North	East
—	pass	pass	1◇
pass	2♣	double	pass
?			

The Alternatives

North's double, following an original pass, indicates a desire to play in one of the unbid suits. If game seems unlikely, I can bid two spades or let the double stand. If I decide to try for game I can jump in spades or make a more scientific approach with two diamonds or three clubs. To bid no trump at any level would surely be misguided, so the alternatives are:

Three Spades
Two Spades
Three Clubs
Two Diamonds
Pass

The Choice

Partner has come in vulnerable at the two level and I feel that he must either be close to an opening bid, with at least nine cards in the majors, or be strong distributionally. Let's begin by looking at a few hands and seeing whether they fit in with his bidding so far.

(1) ♠ K J x x x   ♡ K x x x x   ◇ x   ♣ x x

Not strong enough to risk entry at this point.

(2) ♠ K Q J x   ♡ K Q 10 x x   ◇ x   ♣ x x x

If his distribution is 5 – 4 he will not be weaker than this.
The following hands are nearer to what I would expect:

(3) ♠ K J 10 x x   ♡ K Q 9 x x   ◇ x x   ♣ x
(4) ♠ A J x x x   ♡ Q J x x x x   ◇ x   ♣ x
(5) ♠ A x x x x x   ♡ K J x x x   ◇ x   ♣ x

Putting these hands opposite mine, two things become clear: it
would be a mistake to pass the double, which would be a success only
opposite hand (2), and there are definite chances of game. Thus, we
can eliminate a pass and reject two spades as inadequate.

Two Diamonds would be ambiguous

Of the stronger calls, two diamonds would keep the bidding at a low
level but would be open to misunderstanding. It might look to partner
as though I could not assist in the majors but had a long string of
diamonds and was willing to play in that suit. His own shortage in
diamonds would point to that conclusion. He might take out into a six-
card suit of his own but he would not be wrong to pass on (2) or (3)
above.

Three Clubs more flexible than Three Spades

A jump to three spades would not be far wrong on values but would
sometimes land us in the wrong suit. On hand (4), for example, four
hearts would play better than four spades.

A force of three clubs enables us to bid the hand with greater
accuracy. If partner has longer spades than hearts he will bid three
spades and I will go to game. When he has longer hearts than spades
he will bid three hearts and I will transfer to three spades. He will
know that I am able to stand four hearts as well. When he has equal
length in the two suits, as on hand (3) above, his correct bid technically
will be three diamonds and then again I will bid three spades.

This seems to deal satisfactorily with all possibilities and I mark the
alternatives:

Three Clubs	10
Three Spades	7
Two Spades..	4
Two Diamonds	2
Pass	1

Reflections on the Bidding

It was possible to form a fairly close picture of partner's hand after he had passed originally and then stepped in vulnerable at the range of two when the opponents were still unlimited. Game was seen to be a distinct possibility and three clubs was the best call because it gave the maximum chance of finishing in the longer suit. In situations where trump control is likely to be a factor, it is important to realize that a trump suit divided 6 – 2 is preferable to one divided 5 – 3, and that 5 – 2 is better than 4 – 3.

24. Time to Listen

In a pairs event our side is vulnerable and I hold as dealer:

♠ J 5 4   ♡ A   ◇ 8 7 6   ♣ A K Q 8 3 2

I open **one club,** West passes, and my partner responds **one spade.** This is **doubled** by East. I have to search for the best tactical rebid after the sequence:

South	West	North	East
1♣	pass	1♠	double
?			

The Alternatives

A simple rebid of two clubs or a raise to two spades would sufficiently express the high-card values, but a jump to three clubs is a possibility, and so is a defensive three spades, if one assumes that partner will have a fair suit in this sequence. I could seek to inhibit the enemy by redoubling. Some players might fancy a semi-psychic rebid of 1NT or even 2NT, but at the present vulnerability that seems a doubtful move. If we leave that out, the alternatives are:

Three Spades
Two Spades
Three Clubs
Two Clubs
Redouble

The Choice

When the rebid is affected by an element of competition, one can begin by studying what the hand is worth and then consider the tactical situation.

Had there been no intervention I would have judged the hand worth three clubs in terms of playing tricks. However, I would not bid more than two clubs because, with so many high cards missing, the bidding is likely to continue, and three clubs might excite partner too much. I want an opportunity to show my spade support, so it would be awkward if three clubs were to produce 3NT from partner.

In support of spades I certainly don't consider the hand worth more than a single raise. If hearts are played early, partner will need good spades in order to draw trumps and run the clubs. Equally, the pattern of the hand is not suitable for a ruffing game. There may be hearts to ruff, but not enough entries to the North hand.

Redouble

Turning to the competitive angle, I don't see much advantage in redoubling. The hand has two features I wish to show—good clubs and moderate support for spades—and a redouble would make no progress in either direction. Also, it would be unsound to redouble now and follow with three spades over an opposing three hearts or three diamonds.

Three Clubs

This has some pre-emptive value and expresses the general strength. The only disadvantage is that opponents will probably not be silenced, and I may be faced on the next round with a difficult decision whether or not to contest further with three spades.

Three Spades and Two Spades

The hand is worth so much more in clubs than spades that it seems bad timing to raise the spades now and probably be unable later to rebid the clubs. A jump to three spades is plausible only on the basis that a partner who responds one spade to one club on a moderate hand will necessarily have five spades—the modern style being to respond in a lower suit when possible. Even if one accepts that, nine tricks in spades will still be hard to make when partner holds something like five spades to the Ace plus the King of hearts. East's double makes it seem likely that at least one of the black suits will divide badly.

Two Clubs

This bid gives up any pre-emptive notion but has advantages in the way of accurate expression. Suppose that West bids two of a red suit and this is followed by two passes. Then my rebid of two spades will be just right. If, instead, partner is able to make a free bid of two spades himself, that clears up all problems. If diamonds are bid by West and raised by East, then I will hazard three spades, taking partner to be short in diamonds and so to have some length in the black suits.

A problem will arise only if West bids two hearts, partner passes, and East raises to three. If that happens I shall probably pass, for they may well be on their way to four and I have no intention of defending at that level.

The simple bid, two clubs, enables me to express my hand accurately and also to *listen* so that I can form an idea of how high to go. That seems to outweigh any advantage that can be gained by a mild pre-empt, and I mark the alternatives:

Two Clubs	10
Three Clubs	8
Two Spades..	4
Redouble	4
Three Spades	1

Reflections on the Bidding

Defensive jumps are all very well in their place—which is when you know that your side is outgunned and the only question is how high you dare go to prevent opponents from exchanging information. When, as here, the issue of the hand is uncertain, it can be a mistake to abandon normal development. Three clubs may silence partner as well as the opposition; he will not take it as an invitation to repeat his spades. Still more important, as was stressed above, is that the quiet bid gives you the best chance to gauge the general lie of the cards.

Many players, I think, would overestimate the South hand in support of spades. Compare the original hand with another that has the same high cards and distribution:

(1) ♠J54 ♡A ◇876 ♣AKQ832
(2) ♠J54 ♡6 ◇A87 ♣AKQ832

Hand (2) is much stronger. The entry for the clubs cannot be knocked out so readily; there is second round control of every suit; and if partner has one or two entries such as King of diamonds or Jack of clubs, he may be able to negotiate several ruffs in hearts. Yet for players who witlessly compute their values in terms of high-card and distributional points, the two hands are the same.

PART FIVE

Competitive Decisions

These are mostly competitive hands at the part-score or game level where a decision has to be made whether to pass, double, or bid on. The standard approach, as seen in the first example, is to form an estimate of how many tricks each side is likely to make in its own contract and then to evolve a tactical plan.

25. Off Balance

My opponents in a match-point pairs tournament are enterprising players. With the opposition vulnerable, my partner deals and opens **three spades**. East passes and I contemplate:

♠ J 9 7 5   ♡ K 8 7   ◇ A 9 8 4 2   ♣ 5

If only for defensive reasons, I must raise to **four spades**. West asks for a review of the bidding and studies the duplicate board, as players do when caught off balance. Eventually he **doubles**, North passes and East bids **five clubs**. Now, do I press on? The bidding has been:

South	West	North	East
—	—	3♠	pass
4♠	double	pass	5♣
?			

The Alternatives

If I decide to sacrifice I can go to five spades at once or bid five diamonds on the way in order to put partner more in the picture. On the other hand, it might be a mistake to sacrifice, and perhaps I should pass or even double. If so, the alternatives are:

Five Spades
Five Diamonds
Double
Pass

The Choice

At this point of a competitive auction I like to consider first, "Who is likely to make what?" and second, "What can I do about it?"

As for our own side, the average expectation of tricks opposite an opening three bid is about nine, I would say.

Our prospects in defence are harder to calculate. Generally speaking, holding only an Ace and a King plus length in the suit in which partner has pre-empted, I wouldn't expect to defeat an opposing contract at

228

the five level. However, I mustn't lose sight of the fact that the opponents have not had much time in which to exchange information. West's double was no doubt intended to be optional, and East's five clubs may not suit him particularly well. Opponents who contest against a pre-empt don't always land on their feet.

If I had to make the final decision over five clubs I would go to five spades, but partner is still there and I feel I ought not to prejudge the issue.

There is another reason for letting them play five clubs, assuming that partner does not defend. This may not be the only game they can make and five clubs may not produce a good score in match points. There is no guarantee that *every* North player will open three spades, and some East-West pairs may have a clear run to a game in hearts or even notrumps.

Wrong to double

There is no point in doubling five clubs, for if we can beat it we shall make a good score anyway. Also, while I am not going to sacrifice, I must not discourage my partner from doing so.

Five Diamonds or Five Spades?

As between five diamonds and five spades, five diamonds might assist partner to take the right decision should opponents go to six clubs. I don't think that is very important here, because unless we could beat six clubs we would get a bad score in any event. A sacrifice in spades at the level of six would be too high in comparison with most other tables.

There is a somewhat better reason for bidding five spades rather than five diamonds. This is that the higher call gives West less room for manoeuvre. Over five diamonds West can make a forcing pass, he can double, or he can introduce hearts on a suit such as A Q J x x. If five spades is bid immediately, West will have a sharper decision.

However, this discussion is academic because I don't propose to make either call in front of my partner. I mark the alternatives:

Pass	10
Five Spades	6
Five Diamonds	4
Double	1

Reflections on the Bidding

When this problem was put to a panel of experts the majority vote was for bidding on, several critics making the point mentioned above that five diamonds would assist partner to judge his action over six clubs. As I see it, these answers overlook the practical point that when opponents have begun the exchange of information at the five level, and especially when there has been an optional double, they often arrive in the wrong spot.

Suppose that the auction had been instead:

South	West	North	East
—	—	3♣	4♣
4♠	5♣	pass	pass
?			

Now the presumption that East-West are in their best contract is much stronger, and at the vulnerability the natural action for South would be to sacrifice.

26. A Cheerful Prospect

Playing rubber bridge with a sound partner against average opponents, I hold in fourth position:

♠ — ♡ A 8 7 4 ◇ A K J 9 7 5 4 ♣ J 3

Neither side is vulnerable and West, on my left, opens **one heart**. My partner overcalls with **one spade** and East bids **two hearts**. I have to find a strategic call after this sequence:

South	West	North	East
—	1♡	1♠	2♡
?			

The Alternatives

I could bid a number of diamonds from three to five. I could double two hearts and I might step out with 3NT. That seems to be all, so the alternatives are:

Five Diamonds
Four Diamonds
Three Diamonds
3NT
Double

The Choice

Although I am void in the suit my partner has called, there are hopeful prospects. We might catch them for a penalty in hearts or we might score a surprise game.

A Double premature

I shall look for a move that retains at any rate one of those possibilities. The first call to reject is a double. That would be decidedly premature. We might set them one trick, though even that is not certain, and we would be missing the chance of better things.

Diamond raises

Five diamonds would not be a bad gamble on the values held.

Partner is presumably short of hearts and can reasonably be expected to have some support for diamonds. However, my hand contains only eight playing tricks in diamonds, counting no losers in the trump suit. If we can make eleven tricks, partner should be able to raise four diamonds to five. Four diamonds expresses the value more accurately, and the possibility remains that West, with some sort of heart-club two-suiter, will bid four hearts.

Three diamonds has a better chance of attracting competition, though probably not beyond the range of three. If three diamonds is passed out I shall make overtricks; perhaps too many.

A fair gamble

There remains 3NT, a call that becomes more attractive as one examines it. If the diamonds are solid, then nine tricks at notrumps should be easier than eleven in diamonds. Partners don't always have the singleton heart you look for, and against five diamonds the opponents may lead an early trump.

I must think what might happen after 3NT. Well disciplined partners seldom take back into four spades after this sort of sequence, but if he does that I shall have to go five diamonds. On the other hand, partner might take out into four clubs on a black two-suiter; then he should subside over four diamonds. Finally, I expect 3NT to be doubled by East on the strength of his spade holding. If that happens I shall give him the lash with a redouble.

Having persuaded myself that this is a promising venture, I mark the alternatives:

3NT	10
Four Diamonds	6
Three Diamonds	6
Five Diamonds	4
Double	1

Reflections on the Bidding

The problem here is not so much to recognize the merits of 3NT as to think of the call in the first place. Such a bid after the opponents have opened often has a surprise effect. 3NT redoubled and made with an overtrick is not at all an unlikely outcome at rubber bridge!

27. From Four Sides

Playing rubber bridge with a partner who is not shy in competitive situations, I hold as dealer:

$$\spadesuit K74 \quad \heartsuit J1043 \quad \diamondsuit 1082 \quad \clubsuit KQ10$$

With neither side vulnerable I pass and West, on my left, opens **one spade**. My partner overcalls with **two diamonds** and East comes in with **two hearts**. What action, if any, should I take after the bidding has gone:

South	West	North	East
pass	1♠	2◊	2♡
?			

The Alternatives

I have the values for a raise in diamonds and perhaps for 2NT. Three clubs, to attract an advantageous opening lead, is a tactical possibility. As opponents are in a forcing position, the best move for the present might be to pass. Nothing else appears plausible, so the alternatives are:

Three Diamonds
Three Clubs
2NT
Pass

The Choice

To say that one has the values for 2NT is one thing; to say that one expects to make it is another. I have a stop of sorts in both their suits, and if West obligingly led away from the Ace of spades and the diamonds were solid I might make several tricks. It is theoretically possible for partner to hold:

$$\spadesuit xxx \quad \heartsuit x \quad \diamondsuit AQJ9xx \quad \clubsuit Axx$$

Even then, if West led a heart, a spade return through my King would be disastrous. I think it would be foolish to press for game at notrumps. With an Aceless hand like mine there is seldom time to develop nine tricks.

Unwise to compete

Three diamonds is a different proposition to the extent that we might well make it. My club honours should be useful. However, there are several points that can be raised against immediate competition:

(a) Opponents have not so far found a good fit. They may be on their way to a contract they cannot make.

(b) My hand is primarily defensive in type and I certainly don't want to encourage partner to sacrifice at a higher level.

(c) Opponents are in a forcing position. I can pass now and compete on the next round if West calls two spades and that is passed to me.

(d) If I bid three diamonds now and West becomes declarer at spades, partner may make an unfortunate lead such as Ace of diamonds from A Q.

Three Clubs for a lead?

This last possibility could be averted by my calling three clubs now instead of three diamonds. Such a call is often good tactics when one is certain that the opponents will bid on, but here I might well be left to play in a silly contract.

Virtue in a pass

Having criticized the other calls we remain with a pass, and that does indeed seem to be the best action. I can bid later over two spades without any fear lest partner continue the defence at an inauspicious level. Three diamonds is best of the other calls because if it buys the contract it has a fair chance of being made. I mark the alternatives:

Pass	10
Three Diamonds	6
2NT	3
Three Clubs..	3

Reflections on the Bidding

Can you, without looking back, recall the four arguments put forward against the immediate raise to three diamonds ? They represent useful lines of thought when a close competitive decision has to be made.

Note: Suppose that South passes, as we suggest, and the bidding takes this course:

South	West	North	East
pass	1♠	2◇	2♡
pass	2♣	pass	pass

Now should South reopen with 2NT or with three diamonds?

2NT is better because it leaves partner with more scope for judgment. If he has something like Q x x in spades he will pass 2NT, but if he has a singleton he will remove it.

28. The Pressure Call

In a pairs contest our side is vulnerable and my partner deals and opens **one diamond**. East passes and my hand is:

♠ A J 6 5 ♡ K J 8 6 4 ◇ 8 3 ♣ J 7

I respond **one heart** and West comes in with **one spade**. North bids **two diamonds** and East **two spades**. It seems a delicate question how far we should go in this part-score battle after the sequence:

South	West	North	East
—	—	1◇	pass
1♡	1♠	2◇	2♠
?			

The Alternatives

To bid at all on my hand might transfer a plus score into a minus, so there is a case for passing. I could be bolder and double two spades. The two most likely forms of positive action are 2NT or a raise in diamonds. To repeat the hearts at the three level would be unthinkable, so the alternatives appear to be:

Three Diamonds
2NT
Double
Pass

The Choice

I will begin by applying my first test on close competitive hands. On the evidence to date, who is likely to make what?

If two spades were passed out, I would expect it to go down one or two tricks. If I double, they won't be down more than one. Either way is worth 100 and will not produce a good score if we can make three diamonds or 2NT.

Next, what are our prospects in diamonds? If the bidding by our side had been simply one diamond—one heart—two diamonds, I would have passed and expected North to make it. In the present sequence North has made a free rebid over one spade, and we are vulnerable, so he must have better than a minimum opening and probably a good six-card suit. He is likely to have a singleton spade on the bidding. Two hearts and four clubs might make up his hand, but that is mostly guesswork.

A contract of three diamonds might depend on finesses, but on the whole I would expect it to make. My Jack of clubs may well be a useful card.

I am rather less sanguine about 2NT. I can imagine a spade lead to the Queen forcing my Ace, and then I would have to take tricks quickly. I reckon that if the cards lie well enough for 2NT, three diamonds will also be on, but the converse by no means applies.

Having formed this general picture of the prospects in various contracts, we are in a better position to study the tactical merits of the various calls.

Pass

Not a mistake, and in a different setting—say at rubber bridge with a less-than-expert partner—it would be the soundest course. Partner is still there and may be able to contend further; if he does not, then two spades will probably be defeated. However, in a pairs contest one has to press on these borderline hands, and to accept 50 points or so could be a poor result.

2NT

This presents a fair picture, it might be made, and partner can always take back to three diamonds or possibly try three clubs. A slight disadvantage to the call is that it warns opponents not to contest with three spades—and if they do, they will know where the cards are.

Double

Much too close for my liking, and it violates the general principle that one should not start to double opponents until one has gone to the limit in one's own suits. If opponents were vulnerable, so that a one-trick penalty would be worth 200, the double, though still risky, would stand to gain much more.

Three Diamonds

The disadvantage of this call on the surface is that it might go down when we could have defeated two spades. However, it is arguable that if the cards lie badly for us in diamonds they will lie well for the opponents in spades. Three diamonds has the advantage over 2NT in that it is more likely to stimulate competition. An opponent who has three diamonds may judge that his partner has a singleton and may be disappointed. If East-West go to three spades we will have a good chance of doubling them for 300, a relevant point being that a double at that stage would not reveal the trump holding in the same way as a double at the range of two.

Some of the other calls are not bad, but three diamonds is the "pressure bid," and I mark the alternatives:

Three Diamonds..	10
2NT	6
Pass	5
Double	2

Reflections on the Bidding

The suggested bid of three diamonds here may seem to run contrary to the general advice not to be too competitive on primarily defensive hands. That advice holds good only when it is clear that your side is going to be outbid at the finish—that the hand "belongs" to the opponents. Suppose that in this example South's hand had been:

♠ 10 x   ♡ Q 10 x x x   ◇ K x x   ♣ J 9 x

The bidding has gone the same way:

South	West	North	East
—	—	1◇	pass
1♡	1♠	2◇	2♠
?			

Now three diamonds, though likely to go down one or two, is not immediately dangerous because opponents, lacking a trump trick, will scarcely be in a position to double. The bid is pointless, however, because you cannot expect your side to contest the hand to advantage. By bidding three diamonds you simply help the enemy to judge their prospects better.

Reverting to the original hand, a possible criticism of three diamonds is that it might encourage partner to bid four diamonds over three spades. However, a good partner would make that bid in front of you only if he were sure of his ground; and if the bid of three spades came on your right, you would be in first with a double.

29. They Strike First

In a team event East, on my right, opens **one heart**. Neither side is vulnerable, and I hold:

♠ K Q 10 7 5 3   ♡ 8   ◇ 4   ♣ Q J 9 3 2

We play two spades as a strong overcall and the suit is not good enough for a pre-empt of three spades, so I bid simply **one spade**. West raises his partner to **four hearts** and my partner **doubles**. East passes and I have to judge whether to let the double stand after the sequence:

South	West	North	East
—	—	—	1♡
1♠	4♡	double	pass
?			

The Alternatives

I can leave the double in or take it out into four spades or five clubs. Clearly there is nothing to consider beyond the three alternatives:

Five Clubs
Four Spades
Pass

The Choice

This is the sort of decision that wins or loses matches and it may be helpful to examine the arguments on either side. Players who take out the double reason along these lines:

Partner will assume I have one or two defensive tricks, but my long suits may be worth nothing to him in defence against four hearts. On the other hand, four spades won't go down badly. If I can find him with one or two important cards such as the Jack of spades, the King of clubs, and an Ace, I may even make it. I expect him to hold high cards rather than trumps for his double, for in a situation where opponents are clearly marked with length in their trump suit, the double is co-operative in principle. He is telling me that he has some "tops" and he expects me to use my judgment in deciding whether to pass or bid four spades. Obviously four spades is the better proposition.

The vision these players form is of partner holding something like:

(1) ♠ A x   ♡ x x x   ◇ A 10 x x x   ♣ K x x

With this hand opposite, four spades would be unlucky to fail and four hearts would perhaps go down one trick.

A less optimistic assessment would be that both four spades and four hearts would be defeated 60 per cent of the time, but that the lesser risk would be to defend in spades.

The argument on the other side runs like this:

I am not altogether happy about the double of four hearts, for I realize that they may make it if my partner's values include ♣ A K. However, I don't see that I am in any position to reverse my partner's decision. When I overcall at the level of one I don't promise anything much in the way of defensive tricks and if my partner is short of spades my hand may be useful. I realize he can't have tricks in hearts, but he may have enough trumps to be a nuisance. If his only values were top cards in the side suits, and he had a little support for spades, I would expect him to stretch a point and bid four spades with minimum trump support rather than double and warn me against bidding on. At a low level I would take out a double of hearts, but at this level I must trust him and pass.

The pass would certainly be right if North's hand were more of this type:

(2) ♠ x   ♡ 10 9 x x   ◇ K Q 10 x x   ♣ A x x

Now four hearts, with the enemy trumps 4 – 4, would surely be defeated while either four spades or five clubs our way could be a disaster.

The crucial question is: which of these two hands is North more likely to hold for his double?

Obviously, hand (2), and that seems to me almost the entire answer. On hand (1) most players would pass. They would hope to defeat four hearts but would certainly not want to discourage their partners from defending in four spades. An imaginative North might even bid four spades, judging that partner must have overcalled on length.

The case for Five Clubs

Five clubs is not a likely solution, but let us admit that it could be right if partner had doubled on either of these hands:

240

(3) ♠ x ♡ A x x ◇ J 10 x x x ♣ A 10 x x
(4) ♠ — ♡ 10 x x x ◇ A x x x x ♣ K 10 x x

However, these examples have to be carefully constructed and on most occasions it would be as well to play in four spades as five clubs even if partner had more clubs than spades. There is the further point that one can always bid four spades and test the reaction before venturing on five clubs.

Summing up

My preference for passing is based on two considerations:

1. Both in the short run and the long run, I don't like to cross partner's intentions when he has a better view of the whole situation than I have.

2. In my experience, there is no reason to be pessimistic about the chances of beating four hearts. I hold the black suits, partner is likely to have values in the red suits. If I lead a trump, as I intend to, they may be short of tricks.

To rescue into four spades would be, to say the least, untrustful, and to rescue into five clubs not far short of desperate. I mark the alternatives:

Pass	10
Four Spades	4
Five Clubs	2

Reflections on the Bidding

There are many players who, especially at rubber bridge, will invariably take out a double when they have a two-suiter like this. A curious fact is that they always strike first in the post-mortem (after losing 300 instead of gaining it) by saying, "I couldn't leave it in when you doubled." They don't seem to see the absurdity of saying, in effect, "If you had passed four hearts, expressing no opinion, I would have passed too. When you doubled, indicating that you thought we could beat it, I had to bid four spades."

If partner had passed four hearts it would not have been unreasonable to defend with four spades. When he doubled, that surely should have inclined South to the opposite course.

30. Paper Puzzle

My partner at rubber bridge is an enterprising bidder but not a rash one. We are vulnerable, the opponents not, and in third position I hold:

♠ 9 3   ♡ J 10 4 2   ◇ K Q 6   ♣ 7 5 4 2

My partner opens **one spade** and East overcalls with **two hearts**. I pass this, West raises to **three hearts,** and now my partner comes in with **four diamonds.** East goes on to **four hearts** and I have what seems a close decision to make after the sequence:

South	West	North	East
—	—	1♠	2♡
pass	3♡	4◇	4♡
?			

The Alternatives

If I decide to support my partner the obvious call is five diamonds, but four spades might also be playable. With my trump holding I could double four hearts. If none of these appeals, I can pass the decision up to my partner. There are four alternatives:

> Five Diamonds
> Four Spades
> Double
> Pass

The Choice

The standard question—"Who, on the evidence so far, is likely to make what?"—is difficult to answer here. I imagine that we can defeat four hearts by a trick or two, but our prospects in spades or diamonds are by no means clear.

Partner has not opened with a two bid (as in our system he would with a very powerful two-suiter) but he has bid to the level of four on his own, vulnerable. No doubt he has ten or eleven cards in spades and diamonds. On the surface, if he is 6 – 5, the long suit should be spades, but I don't regard that as certain. Players often open one spade on a hand such as:

(1) ♠ A K J x x   ♡ —   ♢ J 10 8 7 x x   ♣ A x

The fact that partner has bid four diamonds, not three spades, does suggest that he may hold better diamonds than spades. But no doubt he could also hold:

(2) ♠ A Q J x x x   ♡ x   ♢ A J 10 x x   ♣ x

Now we would have a rather better chance in four spades than in five diamonds.

If he has only five cards in each suit he will be somewhat stronger, such as:

(3) ♠ A K Q x x   ♡ x   ♢ A J 9 x x   ♣ K x

Assuming that I intend to make either call, it is not easy to decide between four spades and five diamonds. If partner has only five spades, then a contract of four spades will be extremely hazardous unless the spades are as strong as in example (3).

Any spade or diamond contract will fail if the suits break badly. It is probably right to say that if they can make four hearts, owing to freakish distribution, we would be doubled and perhaps heavily defeated in either of our contracts.

That seems to be the deciding factor. Take this likely sort of hand for partner:

(4) ♠ A K x x x x   ♡ —   ♢ A J 10 x x   ♣ Q x

If the adverse spades are 3 – 2 we can make four spades, barring an unexpected accident such as a trump promotion. But if the spades are 4 – 1 we will still have a good chance to make four tricks in defence. In short, this is not one of those hands on which there might be game for both sides. It is a hand where, if by chance we cannot beat four hearts, we shall certainly be down in four spades.

Double or pass?

Though it didn't seem obvious at first, I am fairly clear in my mind now that it would be a mistake to bid either five diamonds or four spades. I expect to defeat four hearts, but I am not sure that I ought to double in front of my partner. If he is 6 – 1 – 6 – 0 or has any powerful hand on which he will be bidding four spades if I pass, I am more than content that he should do so. He would have to respect a double on my part, because all my values could be in hearts and clubs. If I pass we may score 100 instead of 300, but if I double we may set them one trick instead of making a game. As it may be wrong to commit our side to a definite course either way, I mark the alternatives:

Pass	10
Double	8
Four Spades	5
Five Diamonds	5

Reflections on the Bidding

When this problem was put to an expert panel, there were 6 votes for five diamonds, 5 for four spades, and a lone voice (mine, though I now consider a pass to be more accurate) for double.

I have a feeling that these eleven votes for supporting partner were "paper answers." That is to say, at the table, with a sure trump trick and a promising line of defence (the lead should be King of diamonds) many of these players would prefer to defend rather than place such stress on partner's vulnerable bidding.

My own view is that at this level it is usually easier to make four tricks in defence than ten or eleven in attack and that to press on is essentially the "expert's error."

31. Deceptive Cost

Playing rubber bridge with a partner whom I do not know well but who seems to play a fair game, I hold in fourth position:

♠ A K Q 9 8 3   ♡ 9 5   ◇ J 10 5 2   ♣ 4

The opponents are vulnerable and West, on my left, opens **1NT**. They are playing a fairly strong no trump, about 16 to 18 points. North passes and East raises to **3NT**. My spades are still on the shelf, the bidding having gone:

South	West	North	East
—	1NT	pass	3NT
?			

The Alternatives

I can pass, I can double in the hope of attracting the right lead, or I can defend with four spades. There's nothing else to consider, so the alternatives are:

> Four Spades
> Double
> Pass

The Choice

We can begin, as usual, by trying to estimate who is likely to make what. If I sacrificed in four spades I would expect to make about eight tricks and so lose, on average, 300. Their prospects may depend on the lead, but even if a spade is not forthcoming there is no certainty that they will make the game. Partner may hold clubs, for example, and by the time he comes in I shall have had a chance to signal.

At duplicate scoring, if you judged that they might well make 3NT it would be right to sacrifice, but at rubber bridge it is a bad bargain to accept a likely 300 loss defending against a questionable game. Even if I had a guarantee that I would be only down one, I wouldn't sacrifice here.

What would a Double mean?

The important question is, would partner interpret a double as a request to make an unusual lead, and would he pick the right suit?

One doesn't double on a scattered 15 points in this position, so it seems logical to treat the double as lead-directing, no doubt based on a suit that one hopes to run. Partner should choose his shortest suit, and if he has equal length in spades and diamonds he should choose the spade lead because when opponents bid to 3NT without any exploring they are more likely to have length in the minors than in the majors.

Balance of advantage

Assuming for the present that partner will interpret the double as I want him to, let us examine some other aspects and see where the balance of advantage lies.

At best, the double will gain 1,000 points or so, if as a result of the spade lead they go down 500 instead of making the game. (I trust that I don't have to explain to present readers that the value of the second game, including the trick score, is about 500—not the 800 that goes down on the score-sheet, for that includes the unseen value of the first game.)

I realize that my spades are not necessarily solid. As West has opened a strong notrump with no top honour in spades, he may have J x x x or an equivalent guard. But even then the spade lead may be a good defence. At least partner will have been deflected from the calamitous lead of a low club from, say, Q 10 x x.

They may redouble. I can consider that when it happens and whence it comes. Retreat to four spades will still be available.

With a doubleton spade and a singleton diamond partner may make the wrong choice. Unlucky!

As I said at the beginning, I don't know my partner well and he may not get the message at all. If he makes his natural lead they may end up with three doubled overtricks. Oh well, I shall have a new partner for the next rubber. So will he!

I mark the alternatives:

Double	10
Pass	5
Four Spades	2

Reflections on the Bidding

One of the commonest mistakes in competitive bidding is to overcall in this sort of situation. When players go off 300 only to find they could have defeated the opponents, they shrug it off with the remark, "I knew it couldn't cost much."

In fact, they have lost 350 or 400 points by bidding on instead of passing or doubling. Had they been right, in that opponents would have made their game, the gain at rubber bridge is only about 200. So before embarking on a sacrifice of this kind you want to be satisfied that the odds are two to one on their being able to make game.

Postscript

The idea that an "unexpected" double of 3NT should be lead-directing is now widely accepted, at any rate among tournament players. It is a good system to treat all unexpected doubles of game contracts as lead-directing, like the lightner double of a slam contract.

32. Dubious Action

In a team event neither side is vulnerable and in fourth position I hold:

♠ 8 5   ♡ K Q 8 7 5   ◇ 3   ♣ A Q J 8 4

West, on my left, opens **one spade**, my partner passes, and East responds **two diamonds**. The question is whether—and if so, how— I should enter the auction after the sequence:

South	West	North	East
—	1♣	pass	2◇
?			

The Alternatives

I can pass for the moment and decide later whether or not to contest. I can come in with a straightforward two hearts, or I can signify my two-suiter by doubling or by bidding 2NT, which partner will take as the "unusual notrump" denoting length in the unbid suits. Thus there are four alternatives:

> 2NT
> Two Hearts
> Double
> Pass

The Choice

When both opponents have shown signs of strength and I have a useful hand, I like to consider first whether there is any likelihood that our side can obtain the contract, other than by way of an unprofitable sacrifice. There doesn't seem much prospect of that here. There is not room for partner to have more than 6 points or so and those would have to be distributed in an exceptionally lucky way for us to outbid the enemy. He might have support for hearts but they would still have the higher ranking suit.

Any action I take will therefore be of a defensive nature. Is it likely that we will have a profitable sacrifice at the five level against four spades? Possibly, but almost surely we would go down 300 to save 420. It is still less likely that it would pay us to sacrifice over 3NT.

We might be able to compete at the level of three, it is true, but that can be achieved by passing now and reopening if West bids two spades and East passes.

Disadvantages of bidding

It looks as though the advantages of positive action are slight. Are there possible disadvantages? Surely! There are three:

(a) You give the opponents a "fielder's choice" between doubling your side or taking a part score or going for game, according to their strength.

(b) Should they reach game despite the intervention they will be assisted in the play. This applies particularly if South makes one of the calls denoting a two-suiter—double or 2NT.

(c) Whatever form of intervention you select, you will be under strength in some respect and that may cause partner to embark on a costly defence. Thus, if you enter with two hearts you suggest a better suit; if with a double, more high cards; if with 2NT, more playing strength.

Best of the others

Of the three forms of positive action, 2NT is the most dangerous in that it forces your side to the level of three. If opponents are not happy about their fit they will take the opportunity to double.

Two hearts has the disadvantage of not telling partner (or the opponents, it is true) that you have equal values in clubs. Also, the suit is weak for intervention in this exposed position. If two hearts is doubled you will have an awkward guess whether to retreat to three clubs.

A double exaggerates the general quality of the hand, but with this call you have a better chance of escaping a penalty.

Summing up

I intend to pass, expecting the hand to develop in one of the following ways:

Opponents will bid game or stop just short. Then I shall be glad not to have given them free information about the distribution.

West will bid two spades. East will pass. Then I shall have a close decision whether to contest with 2NT, but I can meet that problem when it arises.

West will raise two diamonds to three and East will pass. Then I may regret that I did not enter on the previous round. But that is the only time, and I mark the alternatives:

Pass	10
Double	6
Two Hearts	5
2NT	4

Reflections on the Bidding

The point of this example is to emphasize that it is apt to be a mistake to enter the auction when you have little chance of challenging for the contract. One of the popular modern toys, the unusual notrump, is often misused in that way. Say that at equal vulnerability South holds:

♠ x   ♡ x   ♢ Q 10 x x x x   ♣ A 9 x x x

He passes and West, on his left, opens one heart. North passes and East responds one spade. South now thinks, "Ah! Good opportunity to show my distribution! I passed originally so partner will know just what I've got when I bid 1NT."

So he will, but whom will it profit? The opponents, in both the bidding and the play!

33. Mainly Diamonds

Playing in a team-of-four match against first-class opponents, I hold in last position:

♠4 ♡AKJ63 ◊2 ♣AQJ865

With neither side vulnerable, West deals and opens **four spades**. My partner overcalls with **five diamonds** and East **doubles**. A lot of points will depend on my action now:

South	West	North	East
—	4♠	5◊	double
?			

The Alternatives

I can leave partner in five diamonds doubled or I can take the initiative and redouble. If I decide to remove the double I can bid one of my suits or perhaps five spades, requesting partner to choose between hearts and clubs. The alternatives are:

Six Clubs
Five Spades
Five Hearts
Redouble
Pass

The Choice

If we credit West with most of the spade suit there is not a lot for North and East to hold in the way of high cards. Apart from the diamonds there is only the Queen of hearts and the King of clubs.

Who is likely to hold those two cards—North or East? East, I feel sure, must have some strength outside diamonds, for when an opponent has overcalled at the five level the partner of the pre-emptive bidder keeps very quiet on a trump holding such as Q 10 9 x x. At any rate, a good player does, and East is certainly that.

What is left for North to hold?

Diamonds and—diamonds! We have come to the heart of the matter very quickly. Moreover, to bid at the five level with no high cards outside his long suit, North should have seven or eight likely tricks in the suit—not less than A K J 10 x x x or A Q J x x x x x.

What are our chances in Five Diamonds?

We may lose a spade and two diamonds, obviously. But East may have doubled with only one trump trick, expecting to make a diamond, a spade, and another trick somewhere.

Could another suit be better?

It seems unlikely. Suppose you are lucky enough to find partner with, say, 10 x x x of hearts in addition to his diamonds. Since the diamonds are not going to be solid there will still be work to do even in five hearts.

A further objection to any kind of rescue bid is that you cannot be at all sure of making the right one. You might bid five hearts and find that you would have been better off in clubs. If you bid five spades you will arrive at the better of your suits (unless a furious partner can say only six diamonds, which is not unlikely), but meanwhile you have excluded five hearts.

Would a Redouble be a fair venture?

The odds are slightly against. The chances of making or going one down may be about equal, but two down must be adjudged more likely than an overtrick. In addition, if opponents run to five spades the penalty may be 500, but not more.

Nevertheless I prefer a redouble to a rescue and I mark the alternatives:

Pass	10
Redouble	5
Five Spades	3
Five Hearts	2
Six Clubs	2

Reflections on the Bidding

The clue to this problem lay in reflecting that East would not have doubled on trump tricks alone; therefore there was nothing for North to hold but a long string of diamonds.

South's decision would have been more difficult if his opponent had been a poor player or if he could have called his longer suit at the level of five. But even then, with an undisclosed A K and an A Q J and a singleton, should one rescue a partner who has overcalled at the level of five? Please don't do it to me!

PART SIX

Protective Situations

Most partnerships have their own ideas concerning the values for, and meaning of, bids in the protective position. Here we look at a few examples where the sensible call has to be chosen without reference to system agreement.

34. No Surprise

In a team event the opponent on my right deals and opens **one spade**. Both sides are vulnerable and I hold:

♠ A 6 2 ♡ A 10 7 4 3 ◇ A 9 4 ♣ 7 2

Either a double or an overcall of two hearts would be dangerous on this primarily defensive hand, so I pass. West passes also, and my partner reopens with **two clubs**. East bids **two spades** and I have to assess the worth of my hand after the sequence:

South	West	North	East
—	—	—	1♠
pass	pass	2♣	2♠
?			

The Alternatives

On the strength of my three Aces I could bid 2NT or even 3NT. If I take the view that East's vulnerable rebid casts a blight over the prospects of game at notrumps I can introduce three hearts or support my partner's clubs on the doubleton. I might decide that we could beat two spades and chance a double. Three spades (asking partner to bid 3NT if he had a spade stop) would generally take the bidding too high, while a pass would be too feeble, so the alternatives are:

3NT
2NT
Three Hearts
Three Clubs
Double

The Choice

East is vulnerable, he has heard his partner pass, yet he has bid two spades when very much under the gun. He will surely have at least six spades and probably a trick in clubs. In that case even 2NT will be too much.

However, I suppose it is possible for East to have a strongly distributed hand without a top card in clubs. He could have something in the nature of:

$$\spadesuit K Q J 9 x x \quad \heartsuit x \quad \diamondsuit K Q 10 x x \quad \clubsuit x$$

He would bid two spades on this to make it more difficult for opponents to get together in hearts.

But if I place East with that sort of hand, West may be so annoying as to turn up with K x x x or Q 10 x x in clubs. We may still have difficulty in making nine tricks.

It is true that partner can sign off in three clubs over 2NT, but on many hands he will have no reason to do so and 2NT will go down.

The only other approach to game is by way of three hearts. It is possible for partner to hold K J x of hearts or even better, but the odds must be strongly against his being able to bid four hearts. Even three hearts will be a hopeless contract if West holds most of the outstanding length.

Would a Double be sound?

The remaining aggressive action is to double two spades on the grounds that our side must have the balance of the high cards, that East will never be able to enter dummy, and so forth. Against that, there are hundreds of strongly distributed hands on which East will have no difficulty in making eight tricks. It is not as though my hand contained any nasty surprise for him. He *knows* he hasn't got the three Aces!

Is there any merit in Three Clubs?

More than in any of the other calls we have examined. You can expect to make it because there is not much for partner to hold other than reasonably good clubs. It must be better to contest the part score safely than to try for a game that has about one chance in four of succeeding. I mark the alternatives:

Three Clubs	10
2NT	4
Three Hearts	3
3NT	2
Double	1

Reflections on the Bidding

If this bid of three clubs strikes some readers as peculiar or worse,

257

the mote is in their own eyes. I am fortified in that judgment by the fact that when the problem was put to an expert panel, with the Jack of diamonds added in place of the 9, the vote for three clubs was almost unanimous.

The argument relating to a double of two spades is worth noting. South's approach should not be, "How can they make eight tricks against the weight of cards we hold?" Instead he should reflect, "East evidently thinks he won't go far wrong in two spades. What is there in my hand that will come as an unpleasant surprise to him?" The answer to that, obviously, is "Nothing."

35. How will it Play?

With both sides vulnerable in match play, the bidding is opened on my right with **one heart**. My hand is:

♠ A ♡ 8 6 4 3 2 ◇ A J 5 3 ♣ A K J

I don't like trap passes if there is a reasonable alternative, but here I can see none. I pass and so does West. My partner protects with **one spade** and the opener passes. I have to find an intelligent call after this sequence:

South	West	North	East
—	—	—	1♡
pass	pass	1♠	pass
?			

The Alternatives

If you put this problem to ten players you might get ten different answers, ranging from a pass to 3NT.

Two diamonds and three diamonds are possibilities. You might take the view that the hand should play well in spades and so raise despite the singleton. You could give it up as hopeless and let him play one spade. You might try to express the hand by bidding some quantity of notrumps. If we look no further, the list will read:

> Four Spades
> Three Spades
> Two Spades
> 3NT
> 2NT
> 1NT
> Three Diamonds
> Two Diamonds
> Pass

I have not included two hearts because that might be interpreted as showing a heart suit. Being short in hearts himself, partner would be all the more likely to pass.

Let's begin by considering what partner is likely to hold and whether there is any chance of game. Allowing for East's vulnerable opening, there is not much left for North to hold, apart from fair spades and one or two high cards in the minor suits. These are some minimum examples:

(1) ♠ K J x x x x ♡ x ◊ Q x ♣ x x x x

(2) ♠ K J 10 x x ♡ x ◊ 10 9 x x ♣ Q x x

(3) ♠ Q J 9 x x ♡ x x ◊ K Q x ♣ 10 x x

I would not expect him to protect on less than this. Some players do, but that is not our style.

What strikes me at once is that even these moderate hands offer a play for game. Take hand (1), played in spades. Declarer would not draw trumps, of course. After a heart lead he would play to make all the trumps in his hand by ruffing. If he could cash four tricks in the minors, that would be enough.

Little chance for 3NT

Even if we agree that game is possible we still have to get there in co-operative fashion. Which bids can we strike out? All notrump bids, I would say. Apart from the fact that the puny aggregation in hearts may not amount to a stop, we may be cut off from partner's spades. We shall land on our feet only if the spades notrump bid is taken out.

Simple bids such as two spades and two diamonds are harmless but will lead nowhere, for it is most unlikely that partner will have enough to continue. It would be simpler to pass and make sure of a plus score that way.

Four spades, though not so peculiar as it may look, would be unduly precipitous. If partner held hand (3) above, the defence would begin with three rounds of hearts on which West would shed minor suit losers, and four spades would be down at least one, probably more.

There remain for consideration three diamonds and three spades.

What would Three Diamonds mean?

Not long diamonds, surely. With a suit such as A K Q x x x and other values to justify the jump, I would have overcalled on the first round.

Nor will partner take three diamonds to conceal strong support for spades, for with good trump support I would raise directly.

I think he would judge that my spade support was limited, but that I hoped for game in either spades or diamonds. He might place me with a hand of this kind:

♠ K x ♡ K 9 x x ◇ A K J x x ♣ x x

With these defensive values I might pass the opening one heart and it would be natural to follow with three diamonds. If he formed that sort of picture he would presumably jump to four spades if he had a good suit, and if he could raise diamonds he would do so. If he could say no more than three spades I would pass. This seems a fair solution.

What of Three Spades?

I make this a clear second best. With a less-than-expert partner—one who would not draw the right inferences from three diamonds—it would be the first choice.

Assuming a first-class partner, I mark the alternatives as follows:

Three Diamonds..	10
Three Spades	7
Four Spades	4
Pass	4
Two Spades.. .. .. ·..	4
Two Diamonds	3
1NT	2
2NT or 3NT	1

With a moderate player opposite, three spades would be wiser than three diamonds, and the unambitious calls—two spades, two diamonds, and pass—would move up.

Reflections on the Bidding

This problem has been considered by expert panels on both sides of the Atlantic. Many judges said that it was insoluble. Certainly, one cannot be sure of obtaining the best result, but the problem begins to straighten out when one realizes:

That the hand should play well in spades. Even with a five-card suit North might be able to land four spades by way of five trumps and five tricks in the minor suits.

That three diamonds should secure from an expert partner the desired reaction—either a sign-off in three spades, a jump to four spades, a raise of diamonds, or conceivably 3NT.

36. Unreliable Guide

Both sides are vulnerable in a pairs event. In third position I hold:

♠ 532   ♡ 972   ♢ 642   ♣ A K 7 4

My partner opens **one heart** and East overcalls with **one spade**. I don't hold free bids in special awe and if I thought this hand was worth a raise I would produce it, but such virtue as it possesses is more of a defensive nature and I am content to pass. West passes and my partner reopens with a **double**. East passes and the question is whether I should make a constructive call now after the sequence:

South	West	North	East
—	—	1♡	1♠
pass	pass	double	pass
?			

The Alternatives

The possible responses fall into two divisions—the minimum bids (two clubs and two hearts), and the stronger bids (three clubs and three hearts). Another possibility in the latter group is a bid of the opponent's suit. To pass the double, hoping to score 200 on a part-score hand, is the sort of action that only a player who was desperate for a top might take. It's not a call one would normally contemplate, so the alternatives are:

Three Hearts
Two Hearts
Three Clubs
Two Clubs
Two Spades

The Choice

There is no intermediate bid available between the minimum bids and those that look toward game and carry the bidding to the level of three. Thus I must first judge:

(a) Might it be a mistake to go beyond the level of two?

(b) If we settle for one of the safer calls, is there a danger of missing game?

If the answer to both questions is affirmative, I must next consider where the balance of probability lies and other marginal factors.

To arrive at an answer to the first question we will construct some not-so-strong hands on which partner might reasonably reopen, remembering that at match points a player will contest where at rubber bridge he might not.

(1) ♠ A x   ♡ A Q J x   ◇ K J x x   ♣ J 10 x

This wouldn't be pleasant in three clubs or three hearts.

(2) ♠ J x   ♡ A K x x x   ◇ A Q x   ♣ Q x x

Even if the hearts are 3 – 2 there are five possible losers.

(3) ♠ A   ♡ A K x x   ◇ A 10 x x   ♣ J x x x

You might make three clubs, but three hearts would be awkward. Now two hands where game would just about be possible:

(4) ♠ A x   ♡ K Q 10 x x   ◇ A K x   ♣ Q x x

Here partner might pass a response of two hearts, but over two clubs he would go back to the major suit.

(5) ♠ J   ♡ A K x x x   ◇ A Q J   ♣ Q J x x

Now either four hearts or five clubs would be playable. I think he would bid again over two hearts or two clubs from me.

It seems that the balance lies on the side of the weaker call. This was certainly my first impression—that if partner could not speak again over two clubs or two hearts game would seldom be worth bidding. It remains only to distinguish between the bids within the two groups.

The stronger bids

Three clubs could easily be taken for a different type of hand altogether—something like K Q x x x x of clubs and little else.

Two spades has a superficial attraction because it appears to convey some strength and to leave the door open to contracts in either hearts or clubs. However, partner might think that he was being asked to bid 2NT (on a holding in spades such as Q x) or to choose between the two minor suits. Any subsequent bidding would in that case be conducted at cross-purposes.

Among the stronger bids we are left with three hearts, which has in fact some virtues. It makes progress toward the most likely game, and in view of the previous pass it will not be overestimated.

Two Hearts or Two Clubs?

There is not a lot to choose between these two. Hearts score better, but when partner has four cards of each suit more tricks will be made in clubs. The one is as likely to lead to game as the other, for when partner can bid three hearts over two he will also be bidding two hearts over two clubs.

A subtle point that inclines me toward two clubs is this: if the opponents continue with two spades, which is not unlikely as they seem to have eight or nine between them, I am prepared to double if I have already shown my clubs. Partner will know that my defence is limited since I did not bid 1NT before. If his values include Q x x x of clubs he will remove the double. That is a more dynamic plan than bidding two hearts and following with three clubs over two spades, so I mark the alternatives:

Two Clubs	10
Two Hearts	8
Three Hearts	5
Two Spades..	3
Three Clubs	2

Reflections on the Bidding

Many players—good ones among them—would approach this problem from an angle that I consider misleading. They would say, "I have two good tricks and partner will not expect me to have more, as I passed on the previous round. How, then, can it be right to make another weak call? I must jump to three clubs or three hearts."

One answer to that argument is that if you bid simply two clubs and West passes, your partner will not place you with a near-yarborough. It will register on him that the opponents have subsided after one spade.

A more general answer is that the underlying thought—I must tell partner that I have something—is not by itself a reliable guide to the best action. There are, after all, many situations in bidding where it is right to pass equally on zero or 15 points.

The essential question to which South should direct his mind is the one posed above: "If I settle for one of the safer calls, is there much danger of our missing game?"

Postscript

The tendency of modern bidding reinforces the answer to this question. North may be simply "balancing" when he reopens with a double. He is allowing for the possibility that South has passed on a fair hand, probably with good spades. Thus South must not get "busy" on his moderate holding.

PART SEVEN

An Element of Surprise

The common factor among the hands in this final section is that someone at the table has made an irregular call or that there has been, or is about to be, a surprising development.

37. In the Picture

In a team contest our side is vulnerable and in second position I hold:

♠ 9 8 4   ♡ A 10 6 2   ◇ Q 9 2   ♣ K Q 10

East, on my right deals and passes, I pass, and West opens with
one diamond. My partner **doubles** and East **redoubles**. There seem
to be a lot of good hands about, the bidding having gone:

South	West	North	East
—	—	—	pass
pass	1◇	double	redouble
?			

The Alternatives

I can either pass and see what develops or make some call to reflect
my values, such as a jump in hearts or notrumps, or a bid of the opponent's suit. The alternatives are:

2NT
Two Hearts
Two Diamonds
Pass

The Choice

Someone at the table must be bluffing and in all probability it is
West, who has opened in third position. The question that arises now
is whether I should make some bid to clarify the position or pass for
the moment and let the enemy find their own way out of, or into,
trouble.

Possibility of a trap pass

At first sight it seems as though a quiet pass may be the best way to
attract some indiscretion from East. If West passes, my partner, not
knowing what is going on, will bid something and East may step in
with some bid which I can double.

I can think of some weaknesses in that plan. First, if West has made a psychic opening he will take out the redouble—probably into two diamonds—to warn partner that his opening was not serious. Even if that does not happen, East, having redoubled already, will not jump to the skies. The vulnerability is not suitable to a low-level double, so on closer examination there is not much future in the trap pass as such.

The positive disadvantage of passing now is that it will be difficult afterwards to convey to partner the nature of my hand. Also, we shall have to exchange information at a higher level. I would rather look for a bid that will put him in the picture.

Two Hearts a different meaning

Had East passed over the double, a jump to two hearts would have been in order, but after the redouble it would suggest a rather different sort of hand. The presumption would be that the enemy had the balance of the cards and two hearts would sound like an attempt to steal the bid, or prepare for competition, on K Q J x x and not much else.

2NT less accurate than Two Diamonds

An immediate jump to 2NT would carry too great a risk of playing in 3NT with an inadequate holding in the enemy suit. More satisfactory is two diamonds, telling partner that I have a useful hand, but not necessarily forcing to game. Over two diamonds he will perhaps bid two spades; if I then introduce 2NT he will know that my holding in diamonds is sketchy. If he bids two hearts or 2NT I can raise. I see no disadvantage in this call and mark the alternatives:

Two Diamonds	10
2NT	7
Pass	6
Two Hearts	3

Reflections on the Bidding

What happened when this hand was actually played illustrates the danger of being too clever and keeping partner in the dark. South passed the redouble, West (who had opened on A J x x x of diamonds and a Jack) also passed, and North, who had made a minimum double on a 3 – 3 – 3 – 4 hand, deemed it safer to bid a low-level one heart than to climb to 1NT or two clubs. The last thing he expected was a jump in hearts from his hitherto tongue-tied partner. To make it worse, South was so impressed by the need to amend his former abstinence that he jumped to four hearts. This failed by two tricks, while 3NT would have been easily made.

38. Contrary to System

My present opponents in a pairs contest are enterprising players, as will appear in a moment. We are vulnerable and in second position I hold:

♠ A K ♡ Q 9 6 5 4 ◊ 10 5 3 2 ♣ K 3

East, on my right, opens one heart. There's nothing I can say over that, so I pass. West responds two clubs. North passes and so does East. That, of course, is contrary to system. I have to sort out what is happening after the sequence:

South	West	North	East
—	—	—	1♡
pass	2♣	pass	pass
?			

The Alternatives

The natural ways to reopen are 2NT, two hearts or double. Two Diamonds can hardly be right, as we do not want to play in diamonds unless partner can bid them in response to a double. On the other hand, East might be trapping and it might be unwise to reopen at all. The alternatives are:

> 2NT
> Two Hearts
> Double
> Pass

The Choice

East may be trying something new, but in general there are two classes of hand that might account for his opening the bidding and then passing over the response of two clubs. First, there is the out-and-out psychic, probably containing a heart suit, such as:

(1) ♠ x x ♡ K J 10 x x ◊ x x x ♣ x x x

More fashionable nowadays is the semi-psychic opening on a three-card suit with about 10 or 11 points. It could be something of this sort:

(2) ♠ Q 10 x x ♡ A x x ◊ K Q 9 x ♣ x x

This sort of opening can work out well in a number of ways. It may enable East-West to steal the contract on inferior cards, it may take away the opponent's best suit, and it may set a trap when, as on the present occasion, partner's response is in the short suit. When East passes he takes a slight risk of missing game but he knows that he is putting the vulnerable opponents on the spot.

Double or 2NT too dangerous

If East is laying a trap of that sort I will walk right into it if I double. Knowing that his partner has responded at the two level, East will be quick to double any take-out by my partner. Two spades doubled could easily cost 800. To reopen with 2NT would be still more dangerous.

Pass or Two Hearts

The one bid that East will not be able to double if he has opened on a three-card suit is two hearts, and this I am sure is the safest way to reopen. Partner will know that the hearts are a real suit in view of my pass on the previous round.

If East has the other type of hand—just hearts—my partner will have upwards of 12 points and will be able to join in.

However, before taking action that admittedly has its risks, I must consider what sort of result a pass might bring. East, I presume, will not open the bidding at most other tables. I wouldn't open on my hand, but many will. If I reopen now, I won't be any worse off than players who have opened the bidding with one heart. And, of course, there are dangers in passing. If we hold the balance of the cards we will not get a brilliant result by letting them play in two clubs.

I am going to contest with two hearts and I mark the alternatives:

Two Hearts	10
Pass	6
Double	4
2NT	2

Reflections on the Bidding

Most players, I think, would double in South's position, not realizing that this was more dangerous than bidding two hearts.

The semi-psychic opening on a three-card suit and about 11 points is quite a clever manoeuvre. It may buy the contract, or steal the opponent's bid, or trap them into unwise defence. It is a bid that, at rubber bridge, good players often make in a part-score situation.

39. A Quick Appraisal

In a pairs event I am third to speak and hold:

♠ A J 10 5 4   ♡ 4 2   ◇ Q 10 9   ♣ 10 5 2

With neither side vulnerable, my partner opens **one heart** and East, on my right, overcalls with **1NT**. Enquiry from from his partner elicits the information that so far as he knows this is a natural bid. (Some players use an overcall of 1NT as a distributional take-out double.) The customary procedure with my scattered strength is to double the intervention, but from experience on both sides of the table I avoid this call when there is any alternative. Often I have been doubled in 1NT myself and ended with a good result. Knowing that my partner shares this prejudice, I overcall with **two spades** in preference to doubling.

West now bids **2NT**, my partner **three hearts** and East **3NT**. Everyone seems to have a lot of good cards in this sequence:

South	West	North	East
—	—	1♡	1NT
2♠	2NT	3♡	3NT
?			

The Alternatives

I can remedy my omission to double 1NT by doubling 3NT! Having shown some values already, I can pass. Perhaps I should support my partner instead. The alternatives are:

Four Hearts
Double
Pass

The Choice

It is not difficult to judge what is going on. East's notrump bidding is no doubt based on long, solid clubs, and partner has more shape than points. Let's look into the matter more closely and see if we can form an opinion as to how many tricks they are likely to make at notrumps and we in hearts.

Better than a Three Heart opening

To take our side first, the indications are that in playing values my partner has rather better than a three heart opening. My two spades over the 1NT intervention gave no promise of support for hearts, yet he has bid three hearts over 2NT at a moment when he was very much exposed to a double. He must hold a few cards in my suit, I should think, and the rest of his values will be in diamonds rather than clubs—if I am right in assuming that clubs are the basis of the enemy calling.

What are our prospects in hearts?

Quite good, really. My strength appears to be well placed. My doubleton heart represents adequate support in this sequence. East's persistence to 3NT over three hearts suggests a single stop only, for with a double stop he might have preferred to double.

Can we beat 3NT?

We might not. At any rate, I can picture them winning the first heart and running off six or seven clubs. If East has the Ace of diamonds as well, they may make nine tricks before we get started. Looking at it another way, there is nothing in my hand to suggest that East will be disappointed in his evident expectation to go very close to 3NT.

The match-point angle

If I double 3NT and we beat it by one trick, that may not be a good result, for I dare say that some pairs our way will be making 140 or 170 in a part score. I can pass 3NT to my partner but I don't suppose he will be able to do any more. It's for me to make the decision. I am going to bid four hearts and I mark the alternatives:

Four Hearts	10
Pass	5
Double	3

Reflections on the Bidding

When this situation arose at the table I actually held the North, not the South, cards. My partner bid four hearts over 3NT, remarking when he put the dummy down that I had bid three hearts on my own. It turned out well, for the heart hand was:

♠ 9 8 3   ♡ K Q 10 8 7 6 3   ◇ K J 6   ♣ —

East could have made 3NT, and while there was a difficult defence that would have beaten four hearts doubled, in practice we made it.

Not everyone can be so quick on the uptake as to make this four heart bid without much apparent consideration, but when the bidding around the table doesn't seem to "add up," that is the time to stop and work out what is going on.

40. Pleasant Dreams

Most players have their day-dreams, and in one such dream I deal myself at rubber bridge:

♠ — ♡ — ◇ — ♣ A K Q J 10 9 8 7 6 5 4 3 2

My side is vulnerable and the problem is my opening call. To preserve the harmonies I set out the bidding diagram in the usual style:

South	West	North	East
?			

The Alternatives

These will occupy more space than the bidding. Seven clubs cannot be excluded, nor six clubs, nor ... A case could be made for any number of clubs and some would account it clever to pass. We will examine them all:

Seven Clubs
Six Clubs
Five Clubs
Four Clubs
Three Clubs
Two Clubs (conventional)
One Club
Pass

The Choice

Let us be clear about the objectives. To play the hand in seven clubs doubled would be agreeable, but the first objective is to play the hand in clubs, period. Even five clubs undoubled with 150 honours is sweeter than a 300 or 500 penalty against opponents sacrificing at the level of seven.

The possible openings fall into three groups: the big bids (seven clubs, six clubs, and two clubs); the quiet calls (one club and pass); and the deceptive pre-empts (three clubs, four clubs, and five clubs). Let us take these three groups in turn.

The big bids

Seven clubs from hand, vulnerable! They might believe it or they might not, but a defender with a long suit would surely follow the safer course of sacrificing.

Six clubs? A better chance, certainly. If they don't overcall we make a good score, and if they do they may still let me play at the range of seven.

The idea of bidding a conventional two clubs would be to put up a pretence in the later auction that partner's response had improved the hand. This plan might work out well if partner took vigorous action but would fall flat if he had little to say. Meanwhile, the opponents would have a chance to get together and at a high level would be the more disposed to sacrifice.

The quiet calls

If I pass to begin with and then go higher and higher in clubs, vulnerable, will anyone be deceived? Hardly! Opening one club, I shall again be dependent on vigorous action from my partner. If most of the bidding is done by the opponents, they will realize that there is something very strange in the air when I go on bidding and bidding.

The pseudo pre-empts

Three clubs is open to the same objection as the calls in the last group. No one will credit a player who opens three clubs and then tries to play in seven clubs . . .

With the higher pre-empts I stand a better chance. It is not inconceivable that a player who opened four clubs should contest at a higher level. That is even truer of a player who opens five clubs and may have ten or eleven tricks in his own hand, plus honours. After that it would not sound suspicious to follow with six and even seven clubs. There is, however, the disadvantage that if the outstanding strength at the table is equally divided no one may overcall at this level. In this respect there is a big difference between four clubs and five clubs.

Summing up

It is not easy to decide between the bids I fancy—four clubs, five clubs, and six clubs. Six clubs will produce a good score if not overcalled, and there would be nothing suspicious in continuing to seven; but opponents might persist in their sacrifice. Five clubs will work well so long as someone bids over it. Bidding four clubs, I think that, at worst, I will be able to play in five or six clubs doubled. The disadvantage of the lower opening bids is that one may be left with the task of making the running and any deliberate jump will be too obvious a sign of strength. On the understanding that after opening four clubs or five clubs I intend to advance only by minimum stages, I mark the alternatives:

Four Clubs	10
Five Clubs	9
Six Clubs	7
Two Clubs	6
One Club	5
Three Clubs	4
Seven Clubs	3
Pass	3

Reflections on the Bidding

This little fantasy is not without a serious meaning. The point I want to bring out is that when you have an extreme freak and have reason to fear that you may be overcalled at a high level, you must not be impatient, and you must be sure that your tactical underbidding has some verisimilitude about it. To give a more practical example, you hold:

♠ — ♡ — ◇ A J 9 8 7 6 4 2 ♣ K Q 8 6 4

The bidding begins:

South	West	North	East
—	1♠	2♣	2♡
?			

Now it is not clever to pass or attempt some psychic manoeuvre. If you do that, the opponents will realize in time that you were bluffing on a giant. Your objective is to be allowed to play in six or seven clubs, apparently sacrificing. Begin, then, with the sort of bid you might make on a weaker hand. Five clubs would be a good choice.

41. Auxiliary Guard

My partner in a team-of-four match is a good player, but we have not played a lot together. With both sides vulnerable, I hold in third position:

♠ 9 7 6 3   ♡ A J 10 5 3   ◇ A K 10 8   ♣ —

Partner opens **one club,** and the next player passes. I respond **one heart,** and he rebids 1NT. Some players treat a rebid of 1NT as fairly strong, but we have no understanding to that effect, and I take him for a moderate balanced hand of about 13 to 15 points. Even so, I have enough for game. Since a simple change of suit over 1NT would not be forcing, I jump to **three diamonds.** I intend to raise three hearts to four, or to pass 3NT. But partner has another idea—**three spades.** That makes an unusual sequence:

South	West	North	East
—	—	1♣	pass
1♡	pass	1NT	pass
3◇	pass	3♠	pass
?			

The Alternatives

This bid of three spades is open to a number of possible interpretations, such as:

(*a*) North has a fair spade suit which he might have shown on the second round.

(*b*) He is ready to play in 3NT if I have an auxiliary stop, or at any rate some length, in spades.

(*c*) He was much encouraged by the force in diamonds and is making an advance cue-bid, showing the Ace of spades before supporting diamonds.

If I read him for a spade suit I would raise to four spades, and if I thought he was asking for 3NT I would bid that. If I were sure that three spades was an advance cue-bid confirming diamonds, my best bid for the moment would be a return cue-bid of four clubs, taking this opportunity to show the void. The alternatives are therefore:

> Four Spades
> Four Clubs
> 3NT

If it were certain that three spades was an advance cue-bid, agreeing diamonds, then four hearts, showing the Ace, or 4NT as a general slam try, would also come into the reckoning. But for simplicity we will assume that if three spades is definitely an advance cue-bid, four clubs is the best answer.

The Choice

Let us examine the three possibilities above. First, has North a genuine spade suit which he is prepared for me to raise? Suppose he held:

(1) ♠ A J 10 x ♡ K x ◇ Q x x ♣ K x x x

After one club—one heart he might suppress the spade suit for tactical reasons, hoping for a spade lead against notrumps. But having started on that line, would he bid three spades over three diamonds, and, if so, with what object? He would scarcely think the suit worth showing, as a suit, after I had bid two other suits. He would either persist with his original plan and bid 3NT, or he might give false preference to hearts.

It is more likely that he wants to show strength in spades for a different reason, holding:

(2) ♠ A K 10 ♡ x x ◇ Q x x ♣ A x x x x

Now, he might want to convey the message, "If you are worried about spades for 3NT, I hold them well. If you have other plans, this will tell you that I have more honour strength in spades than clubs."

He wouldn't expect me to be able to raise to four spades at this late date. That is another way of saying that three spades is not a game try in spades.

Can he be asking for 3NT?

The second theory was that he might be suggesting 3NT if I could help in spades. For example, he might hold:

(3) ♠ A 10 x ♡ x x ◇ Q J x ♣ A Q 10 x x

He would not expect to make 3NT if I had a singleton spade.
Another possibility of the same sort:

(4) ♠ Q 10 x   ♡ Q x   ◇ J x x   ♣ A K J x x

With so uncertain a guard in the unbid suit he would hesitate to bid
3NT himself, but at the same time would not want to by-pass that
contract in case I held J x or something of that kind. Then there might
be too many top losers in a suit contract.

Both these constructions are possible. 3NT certainly cannot be ruled
out.

Could Three Spades be an advance cue-bid, confirming diamonds?

Possibly. It would be a hand of this type:

(5) ♠ A x   ♡ K x   ◇ Q J x x   ♣ K J x x x

Now three diamonds would excite him and three spades, to be
followed by support for diamonds, would be a sound manoeuvre
With this fit there would be a good play for six diamonds.

However, if that is his intention, he will clarify by bidding four
diamonds over 3NT. Thus, an imaginative four clubs on my part
at this stage is unnecessary and could easily be misread.

The more I look at it the more it seems that 3NT is most likely
what he wants to hear and also will not be fatal if he has other plans.
Even if he has a spade suit we may well make 3NT, and if he is heading
for a slam in diamonds, that is not ruled out by my bidding 3NT. So
I mark the alternatives:

3NT	10
Four Spades	3
Four Clubs	3

Reflections on the Bidding

When partner has made a somewhat ambiguous bid, as certainly
North did here, it is wise to consider not only, "What does he mean?"
but also "What bid can I make that will allow for more than one
possibility?" It is on these grounds that 3NT is clearly right on this
hand. Even if based on a misunderstanding of partner's holding, it
will still not lead to a calamity, as might any of the other bids.

Did you note the inference that led us to conclude that partner had

281

not bid spades as a genuine suit? We reflected that after this sequence he would not expect South to be able to support, so would not bid the suit with that idea in mind.

Glance again at hands (3) and (4) and the suggested bid of three spades. This is a good example of modern tactics in such a situation. If North held the unbid suit strongly enough for 3NT he would make that bid himself. When instead he calls the suit the message is, "If you can contribute a little support in this quarter then we should be in 3NT."

42. Do We Like It?

In a rubber bridge game of high standard the opponents are vulnerable, we are not. East, on my right, opens **one heart** and my hand is:

♠ J 10 4 2   ♡ 9 8 4 2   ◇ K Q 9   ♣ 8 4

I pass, West responds **one spade**, and East rebids **two hearts**. This is passed to my partner, who **doubles**. When East passes, my first task is to decipher the meaning of the double after the sequence:

South	West	North	East
—	—	—	1♡
pass	1♠	pass	2♡
pass	pass	double	pass
?			

North's double could be interpreted in three ways: as a penalty double, which I would happily pass; as a request for one of the unbid suits, to which I would have to respond with three diamonds; or as a hand with all-round strength apart from hearts, in which case two spades would be the most economical response. I can't imagine 2NT being a good bid in any circumstance, so the alternatives are:

> Three Diamonds
> Three Spades
> Pass

The Choice

Partner would not take a foolish risk at this vulnerability, so I can take it that he was strong enough to enter the bidding on the first round but was prevented by some tactical consideration. With a strong minor two-suiter he could have come in over one spade, and with a distributional two-suiter the bid he would choose now is 2NT, not double. Thus I am sure it would not be right for me to bid a three-card minor suit.

Can the Double be for penalties?

Inconceivable, really. To double for penalties, sitting under the heart bidder, he would need a very strong trump holding. East, who has bid hearts twice, must hold five at least, probably six, and I hold four, so there are not many left for partner. He may have a generally defensive hand on which he would be happy to hear me pass the double if I had tricks in hearts, but he himself must be short of hearts.

Has partner length in spades?

That is the natural conclusion from his bidding up to now. It would explain why he did not enter on the previous round. Holding strength in the suit bid on his right, he was waiting to see how the bidding would develop.

Once that inference has been drawn, it becomes apparent that my best bid is two spades. That will work well if partner holds something of this sort:

$$\spadesuit A Q 9 x \quad \heartsuit x \quad \diamondsuit A 10 x \quad \clubsuit Q 10 x x x$$

Such an example is sufficient to point the folly of passing or bidding three diamonds. The bid I dismissed earlier, 2NT, would in fact be less destructive than passing the double, so we should perhaps give it a place in the marking:

Two Spades..	10
Three Diamonds..	4
(2NT	3)
Pass	1

Reflections on the Bidding

When a player fails to overcall on the first round of bidding and reopens later in circumstances that suggest he must hold a good hand, it can generally be assumed that he is strong in the first suit bid on his right.

This problem was set in a bidding competition promoted for its readers by a Belgian newspaper. The panel of experts who answered the questions all interpreted North's double in the sense I have described, and so found the same answer, two spades. Of 5,842 readers, however, no fewer than 4,486 were prepared to pass the double of two hearts. One can only assume that they forgot to ask, "Why did North not bid on the previous round?" and "Can he possibly have the trump strength to make a penalty double at the range of two?"

43. Time for Discretion

In a team event I am fourth to speak and hold:

♠ A63   ♡ J9742   ◇ 106   ♣ K85

Neither side is vulnerable and West, on my left, opens **three diamonds**. My partner overcalls with **four diamonds**, and while I am wondering how to deal with that, East bids **five diamonds**. I enter the auction for the first time at the range of five:

South	West	North	East
—	3◇	4◇	5◇
?			

The Alternatives

In our system, the normal bid for a take-out over three of a minor suit is a double. The overcall in the opponent's suit conventionally denotes a powerful two-suiter. I could pass now to enable my partner to declare himself, I could attempt to express my general values with a double of 5NT, or I could bid five hearts freely. As my Ace of spades and King of clubs are good cards to hold after this sequence, I could also bid six diamonds to extract a choice from my partner, or six hearts. That makes quite a few alternatives:

Six Hearts
Five Hearts
Six Diamonds
5NT
Double
Pass

The Choice

In view of my length in hearts, the most likely construction of my partner's hand is a two-suiter made up of spades and clubs. He would overcall three diamonds with four diamonds on a hand of this type:

(1) ♠ KQ10xx   ♡ Ax   ◇ —   ♣ AQ10xxx

He would plan to bid four spades if I responded with four hearts. He would expect me then to read him for a spade-club two-suiter and to amend to five clubs if I had a singleton spade and three clubs.

I feel that there should be a playable slam somewhere, and my first objective is to discover the nature of his presumed two-suiter. Let us examine the possible calls in turn.

Pass

I could pass five diamonds to see what he would call. Then if he bid five hearts or five spades I could raise to six. If he doubled I could transfer to 5NT, perhaps, and then he would bid one of his suits. This seems a fair solution, but I can think of two small disadvantages. One is that if he had stretched a little to make the overcall of four diamonds he might be unable to bid over five diamonds. The other drawback is that he would not realize I was so strong, and we would have little chance to reach a possible grand slam. If I pass, I am temporarily deceiving him.

Double

Sometimes a double is the only way to indicate some general values, but here it would be misleading. Partner might conclude that I was lacking top cards and was warning him not to persist with his two-suiter.

Five Hearts

I can imagine circumstances in which this bid would put a con-siderable strain on partner. Suppose that he had a fair holding in hearts, such as A 10 or K Q alone. He might reflect that after he had indicated a two-suiter I would not voluntarily introduce a suit of my own at this level unless it were strong. So he might pass and we would play in the wrong suit. Apart from this possibility, the bid would give no picture of my two key cards in the black suits.

Six Hearts

This would be an even worse mistake. Partner would think that my hearts needed little or no support and might leave me in with a singleton.

Six Diamonds

This would convey my strength but has the disadvantage of excluding six clubs. Partner might hold:

(2) ♠ K 9 x x x ♡ A K ◇ — ♣ A Q J 9 x x

Now six spades would be at the mercy of the trump break, while six clubs would be very unlucky to fail.

5NT

Partner will not take this as a natural bid, for if I had a trick in diamonds I would double five diamonds. He will understand it as a general slam try telling him that I can play at the level of six in whatever suit he chooses. This seems clearly best, and I mark the alternatives:

5NT	10
Pass	6
Six Diamonds	5
Double	4
Five Hearts	3
Six Hearts	1

Reflections on the Bidding

The overcall in an opponent's suit at this level to denote a two-suiter is a useful weapon, but it has to be used with discretion. For example, with a two-suiter consisting of spades and hearts it is dangerous to bid four diamonds over three diamonds because partner may have no alternative but to respond with five clubs. For that reason (though this was not mentioned in the discussion above), there was a fair inference for South that his partner's hand contained clubs, and a jump to six clubs would actually be more intelligent than many of the calls listed.

The responder's duty is to bear in mind that his partner has a two-suited, not a three-suited, hand. He must avoid any call such as six hearts in the present sequence which may cut right across partner's intentions.

Postscript

I underestimated the virtue of a double in this discussion. As the bidding has gone, a double would indeed suggest a few high cards and is a better answer than a pass.

44. The Joker

At rubber bridge my opponents are good players and one of them is something of a jester, as events will show. My partner is also a competent player. We are vulnerable and in second position I hold:

♠ A J 9 4 ♡ 5 ◇ K 10 6 ♣ A K Q J 9

East, on my right, opens 1NT. They are playing, in theory, a weak no trump of 13 to 15 points not vulnerable. I double, West passes, and so does my partner. The opener now removes himself to—four hearts! When I recover from the shock, what do I do after the sequence

South	West	North	East
—	—	—	1NT
double	pass	pass	4♡
?			

The Alternatives

I can bid one of my suits, either spades or clubs. 4NT would be an exaggeration and might be misunderstood. I can double four hearts or I can pass and see what my partner will do. The alternatives are:

Five Clubs
Four Spades
Double
Pass

The Choice

East, I assume, has a hand on which he could have opened with a pre-emptive four hearts. It must be a strong hand of that type, because after the double of his psychic 1NT he must realize that he is not going to play undoubled. I should imagine that he has about eight or nine tricks in his own hand.

Not a lot can be inferred from my partner's pass of 1NT double except that he is fairly balanced. Even if quite weak he may prefer defending against 1NT to bidding a poor suit at the two level.

We can probably defeat four hearts, but I doubt whether we can beat it enough to compensate for a vulnerable game. East understands the mathematics of rubber bridge and would not walk into a 500 penalty. 300, less 100 honours, is closer to the mark.

The only conclusion we have reached so far is that a game will be worth much more to us than any penalty we are likely to collect. If I had to choose between the suits I would bid five clubs rather than four spades, but the fact that partner has passed the double of 1NT by no means establishes that we can make eleven tricks in clubs. He need be no better than:

(1) ♠ Q x x ♡ x x x ♢ Q x x x ♣ x x x

Five clubs won't go like a bomb with this hand opposite, especially if the trumps are 4 – 1.

Double or Pass?

Since we are not sure of a game, it may seem at first sight as though we should accept what we can from a double. But if I pass, what will partner do? I think he will take it that a hand good enough to double 1NT is also good enough to double four hearts. In other words, he will treat my pass as forcing. On a moderate balanced hand he will double, but if he has a fair suit he will bid it, realizing that is what I am asking him to do.

(2) ♠ Q x ♡ x x x ♢ A J 9 x x ♣ x x x

With this hand he will bid five diamonds. He will bid four spades with any five-card suit, and also on:

(3) ♠ K Q x x ♡ x x x ♢ Q J x x ♣ x x

My pass at this point will be the same in effect as a take-out double of four hearts. That is just the message I want to convey, and I mark the alternatives:

Pass	10
Double	5
Five Clubs	4
Four Spades	3

Reflections on the Bidding

I came into my club one evening to find a group at the bar hotly disputing this situation, which had arisen during the afternoon game.

"South must double," said one. "Five clubs," said another, and "Four spades," insisted a third, showing clever hindsight, for North's actual hand was:

♠ Q 10 x x ♡ x x ♢ A x x x ♣ 10 x x

Whether on this hand North would have bid four spades after a pass by South is doubtful, I admit. Probably he would double.

The principle that emerges from this example is that when a player has already expressed his values he should not be in a hurry to bid in front of his partner. A forcing pass is one of the most eloquent calls in the game.

45. He's Trying, Too

My partner in a pairs event is an imaginative but not a wild bidder. The opponents are vulnerable and in fourth position I hold:

♠ Q 9 6 3   ♡ Q 10   ◇ A J 10 5 2   ♣ Q 9

West, the dealer on my left, opens **one heart**, North passes, and East raises to **two hearts**. I pass, West bids **four hearts**, and now partner suddenly enters with a **double**. East passes and I have to disentangle the bidding which up to now has been:

South	West	North	East
—	1♡	pass	2♡
pass	4♡	double	pass
?			

The Alternatives

When considered in conjunction with my hand, the bidding is mysterious, but I could take the view that no one had asked me to bid. If the double seemed so unlikely as to demand a rescue, I could take out either into four spades or five diamonds. The alternatives are:

Five Diamonds
Four Spades
Pass

The Choice

On the surface, partner's double is for penalties, but if East-West, who are vulnerable, are bidding normally, it is impossible for partner to have any sort of penalty double. The only solution that makes any sense is that he lacked the strength for a take-out double on the first round but is strong enough in distribution to believe that we can save profitably at the five level. He must be 5 – 4 – 4 – 0, with a hand of this sort:

(1) ♠ K J 10   ♡ —   ◇ K 9 x x   ♣ 10 8 x x x
(2) ♠ J x x x x   ♡ —   ◇ Q 9 x x   ♣ A x x x

He will be prepared for me to pass if I have a couple of trump tricks and no suit, but otherwise he will expect me to rescue.

Four Spades or Five Diamonds?

The only question that remains is whether I should take out into four spades or five diamonds. If the result at most tables is going to be 620 or 650 to East-West, it won't make much difference whether we go down three, or one, or even make our contract! What we must avoid is a 700 loss, which would be fatal. That might happen in four spades if partner held hand (1) and the spades and diamonds both broke badly. Five diamonds, with nine trumps, would almost certainly be proof against 700. However, I don't have to decide that now. I can bid four spades for the moment and judge later whether to retreat to five diamonds. I mark the alternatives:

Four Spades	10
Five Diamonds	8
Pass	2

Reflections on the Bidding

This situation occurred in actual play. North held the second of the two hands quoted above, so that it would have paid to sacrifice in either spades or diamonds.

When the problem was later submitted to a panel of experts, more than half gave a pass as their answer. It is true that the solution is not readily apparent, but as the editor of the feature remarked, truthfully if not elegantly, "Because a problem may seem bizarre at first glance is no reason not to think it through imaginatively."

STAR BOOKS

are available through all good booksellers but, where difficulty is encountered, titles can usually be obtained *by post* from:

**Star Book Service,
G.P.O. Box 29,
Douglas,
Isle of Man,
British Isles.**

1 or 2 books – retail price + 5p. each copy
3 or more books – retail price post free.

Customers outside Britain should include 7p. postage and packing for every book ordered.